CHINA IN THE 21ST CENTURY

WHAT EVERYONE NEEDS TO KNOW®

CHINA IN THE 21ST CENTURY

WHAT EVERYONE NEEDS TO KNOW®

2nd Edition

JEFFREY N. WASSERSTROM

With Contributions by
MAURA ELIZABETH CUNNINGHAM

OXFORD
UNIVERSITY PRESS

OXFORD
UNIVERSITY PRESS

Oxford University Press is a department of the University of Oxford.
It furthers the University's objective of excellence in research, scholarship,
and education by publishing worldwide.

Oxford   New York
Auckland   Cape Town   Dar es Salaam   Hong Kong   Karachi
Kuala Lumpur   Madrid   Melbourne   Mexico City   Nairobi
New Delhi   Shanghai   Taipei   Toronto

With offices in
Argentina   Austria   Brazil   Chile   Czech Republic   France   Greece
Guatemala   Hungary   Italy   Japan   Poland   Portugal   Singapore
South Korea   Switzerland   Thailand   Turkey   Ukraine   Vietnam

Oxford is a registered trademark of Oxford University Press
in the UK and certain other countries.

Published in the United States of America by
Oxford University Press
198 Madison Avenue, New York, NY 10016

The Library of Congress has cataloged the first edition as follows:
Wasserstrom, Jeffrey N.
China in the 21st century : what everyone
needs to know/ Jeffrey N. Wasserstrom.
p.   cm.
Includes bibliographical references and index.
ISBN 978–0–19–539447–4; 978–0–19–539412–2 (pbk.)
1. China—History—21st century.   I. Title.
II. Title: China in the twenty-first century.
DS779.4.W376 2010
951.06—dc22
2009045415
ISBN for 2013 edition: 978–0–19–997496–2

"What Everyone Needs to Know" is a registered
trademark of Oxford University Press.

5 7 9 8 6 4
Printed in the United States of America
on acid-free paper

CONTENTS

5 US–China Misunderstandings   113

ACKNOWLEDGMENTS

(TO THE FIRST EDITION)

I owe debts of gratitude to many individuals, beginning with the students who have taken my classes and the people who have attended the talks on China I've given in some fourteen different countries located on four continents over the course of the last two decades. The questions they have asked me helped me figure out which ones to address in this volume. I am enormously grateful to Tim Bent and Dayne Poshusta at Oxford University Press, and the anonymous readers of the book proposal they solicited, for providing me with guidance in refining my list of questions. I also want to thank Tim, the editor in charge of the project, for his unvarying support, unfailing good humor, and the work he did on tightening up the book's prose; and Dayne, for bringing a sharp set of eyes to the manuscript at a key stage in its development.

I want to thank the following friends and colleagues who helped me greatly by answering my inquiries, listening to me try out ideas, sharing unpublished works, or reading and commenting on one or more chapters at very short notice: Susan Brownell, Tim Oakes, Tim Weston, Lisa Claypool, Susan Fernsebner, Lee Haiyan, Sara Friedman, Benjamin Read, and Kate Merkel-Hess (who deserves a special separate expression of thanks, since various parts of the book were shaped by work she and I did on coauthored commentaries).

Going even further beyond the call of duty (and perhaps even friendship), Vanessa Schwartz, Rob Culp, Peter Zarrow, and Kate Edgerton-Tarpley made time to read entire drafts of the manuscript (again at very short notice) and gave me valuable suggestions about how to improve it.

I am grateful to many colleagues, first at Indiana University and now at the University of California–Irvine, for conversations that have contributed to my understanding of China and the ways that it is similar to or different from other countries. There are too many people to list, but I'd be remiss not to mention Maria Bucur, Jeff Isaac, Jeff Gould, Nick Cullather, Mike Grossberg, John Bodnar, Sue Tuohy, Scott O'Bryan, Scott Kennedy, Jeff Veidlinger, Ben Nathans, Mark Roseman, Kumble Subbaswamy, and Michael Curtin (among those formerly or still at IU) as well as, at UCI, Ken Pomeranz, Vinayak Chaturvedi, Bob Moeller, Emily Rosenberg, Yong Chen, Guo Qitao, Dorothy Solinger, Laura Mitchell, Kavita Philip, and Jennifer Munger.

I also want to thank everyone involved with the "China Beat" blog, which was launched at UCI in January 2008. Participating in that venture has provided me with an invaluable continuing education, both about the PRC and about writing, while also offering a wonderful example of what can be accomplished by a group ready to blur or ignore completely the divides that separate, often unnecessarily, the work done by graduate students as opposed to faculty members, academics as opposed to freelance writers with a scholarly bent, and so on. I am grateful to all the "China Beat" contributors (too numerous by this point to list), and especially to Kate Merkel-Hess, Ken Pomeranz, Maura Cunningham, Miri Kim, and Susan McEachern for being such good collaborators on the blog and the related book, *China in 2008: A Year of Great Significance*, which grew out of it.

I owe a special thank you to Nicole Rebec, for giving a complete early draft of this book a careful and thoughtful read for style. And I am very grateful to Nancy Toff, for first getting me involved in the operations of OUP's wonderful New York office.

I want to thank as well Pankaj Mishra, Geremie Barmé, Timothy Garton Ash, Alec Ash, Prasenjit Duara, Harriet Evans, Mark Selden, Timothy Weston, Mary Gallagher, Liz Perry, Gail Hershatter, and Barbara Mittler for conversations or e-mail exchanges we had during 2009 on issues associated with topics covered in this book, which they may by now have forgotten but that shaped my thinking on key issues. In the acknowledgments to an earlier book, I thanked the editors at various general interest periodicals whose comments on short pieces I had worked on for them helped me make the transition from writing just for academics to writing for the public at large. I remain in their debt, and I now want to add a few new names to that list: Joan Connell, Josh Burek, Kate Palmer, Liam Fitzpatrick, Colin McMahon, and Nick Goldberg.

I am grateful as well to Michael Freeman, the inspiring teacher who taught me the first things I ever "needed to know" about China, back when I was a freshman. And the final person I want to thank is, as always, Anne Bock—for the usual reasons, plus in this case for all she does to help keep me aware of the difference between things that "everyone needs to know about China" and things that I simply find interesting about the country.

(TO THE NEW EDITION)

This new edition would not be appearing were it not for the efforts and goodwill of two people. One is Tim Bent of OUP, who has been a tireless supporter of the book from day one and green lighted the idea of updating it. The other is Maura Elizabeth Cunningham, who graciously agreed to join me in the sometimes daunting task of writing new material dealing with the dizzying swirl of events that took place in China during the years following the first edition's appearance. I owe her a very large debt of gratitude; she more than earned the "With Contributions By" credit she has on the title page, and along with all she did on the new questions and answers that are found sprinkled through later chapters, she did much to improve the flow of earlier parts of the book.

I am grateful to many other people as well, including all of those (too numerous to mention) who helped arrange book talks after the first edition appeared, as the questions I got during those events, as well as from the savvy radio interviewers who had me on their shows to talk about the book, sometimes made their way into this updated work. In addition, I want to thank Christian Purdy at OUP, who did a great job publicizing the first edition and has shown a similar commitment to getting the word out about this one; the Chinese studies graduate students at UC Irvine, who have listened to and offered constructive criticism of my interpretations of recent events; Jeremy Friedlein and others at CET Academic Programs, who have helped me get to China regularly; Jon Wiener, who has been as good a colleague as anyone working the borders between academic and popular writing on the past and present could wish for; and the Asia Society, the National Committee on U.S.-China Relations, UCI's Literary Journalism Program, *the Los Angeles Review of Books*, *Dissent* magazine, and the Shanghai International Literary Festival for being such energizing organizations with which to work. Finally, the following people deserve a shout-out for doing everything from sharing their thoughts on China with me to in a few cases co-writing essays with me, or organizing events that proved particularly pivotal in helping me come up with the questions and answers that appear on the pages that follow: Ian Johnson, Angilee Shah, Louisa Lim, Rachel Beitarie, Stephen Platt, Susan Jakes, Evan Osnos, Tom Mullaney, Rob Schmitz, Kaiser Kuo, Jeremy Goldkorn, Mengfei Chen, Tania Branigan, John Ruwitch, Niko Pfund, David Moser, Lijia Zhang, Annie Tully, Lisa Movius, John Flower, Paul French, Lynn Parisi, Karla Loveall, Victoria Augustine, Li Ling, Helena Kolenda, Dan Washburn, Tina Kanagaratnam, and Mei Fong.

AUTHOR'S NOTE

When I took my first class in Chinese history in the late 1970s, signing up for it on a whim, getting a clearer sense of the past and present of the world's most populous nation seemed purely optional, in a way that it no longer does. At the time, I had only a passing familiarity with Chinese culture, politics, and society. This was partly because reports about China made it into network newscasts (then still a very influential medium) only when something very extraordinary happened, such as when President Richard Nixon made his historic trip to Beijing in February 1972. Stories about the People's Republic of China (PRC) only rarely made it onto the front pages of English-language newspapers and almost never appeared in the sports, business, or entertainment sections.

What a difference thirty years can make in the life of a country—and in the degree of global interest it generates. Stories about the PRC now show up in Western newspapers routinely and appear in every section. Moreover, reports about Chinese topics are staples in other kinds of media, from CNN broadcasts to online venues such as the Huffington Post to satiric publications like The Onion, which several years ago devoted an entire issue to musing on how their coverage of the world would change if a Chinese firm bought it.

And yet, as Timothy Garton Ash has noted, we readers in Western countries still get much less thorough coverage of

China than we need, given how complex the country is and how looming its role in global economic and diplomatic affairs has become.[1]

We now live in an era when China has more millionaires, more cities with populations exceeding 1 million, more Internet users, and more skyscrapers than any other country. It figures centrally in the most pressing issues of our day. China produces more greenhouse gases than any other nation. It has vast holdings of US treasury bonds and its factories fill the shelves of the world's big-box stores. China not only has the bomb, but it also maintains a special relationship with North Korea, a country whose nuclear ambitions are a source of grave concern in the West.

Given all this, the need for a primer on China was already self-evident when I set about writing the first edition of this book in 2009. And the course of Chinese and international events since then has only heightened the sense that, for anyone who wants to be seen as an informed global citizen, there remains an urgent need to get a fix on the history, present state, and future prospects of a country that is still the world's most populous (though India may soon wrest that honor—and burden—away from it) and in 2010 surpassed Japan to become the world's second-biggest economy (and, many now assume, destined to overtake the United States). The way that China is developing and being influenced by other parts of the world and how it, in turn, is influencing other nations is a matter of widespread fascination and deep concern. How China fares in the 21st century matters to everyone on the planet.

I was pleased with the response to the first edition of this book, including interest abroad that led to it being translated into Turkish and Korean, but I was very happy to be given an opportunity to revise and update it. And happier still that I was able to persuade Maura Elizabeth Cunningham to collaborate with me on this edition, as she is a talented writer and deeply versed in Chinese history and culture. Maura and I coauthored magazine pieces, and I served as an advising editor to the "China Beat" blog throughout the years she was its chief editor. In preparing this new edition, Maura made suggestions on style that improved the flow of early chapters. She was also an equal partner—and sometimes considerably more than that—when it came to posing and providing answers to new questions relating to the flurry of exciting, distressing, and sometimes bewildering events that have taken place since the first edition went into production.

Even a simple précis of some of these new questions reminds us of how eventful the last few years have been for China. Added to this edition are discussions of Liu Xiaobo's getting the Nobel Peace Prize and Mo Yan becoming a Nobel literary laureate—and the contrasting responses to these awards internationally and in China. Bo Xilai, who was not mentioned at all in the first edition, comes into the picture here via an account of the scandal that brought him down, a scandal that preceded and somewhat deflated the transfer of power from Hu Jintao to Xi Jinping several months later. These and other specific post-2009 events and people are the focus of new questions and answers. So, too, are recent trends, such as the increasing importance of quality-of-life protests and cover-ups that generate intense Internet chatter and undermine the Communist Party's credibility. Last but not least, the new edition comes with a thoroughly updated set of suggested further readings.

Many things about the book have not changed. We could not let go of the cover photos, for example, since they perfectly evoke the sense of a country that has been changing rapidly in some realms and yet surprisingly resistant to transformation in others. Also remaining unchanged is one central goal of this book, which is to help normalize discussions of China, a country that is too often seen as—to use the cliché—inscrutable. Its guiding aim remains to clear up sources of Western misunderstanding about China, provide insights into significant issues relating to it, and, above all, reveal that, though the country can be dauntingly complex, we can arrive at a basic understanding of its nature.

Also unaltered is the basic structure of the book and the kinds of experiences and reading that inform its arguments. It begins with several chapters on China's past and the relevance of this history for contemporary dilemmas, and then concludes with several that zero in on China's present. Maura and I have drawn on research we have conducted and trips to China we have made—in Maura's case several extended stints in the country over the last decade, in mine a yearlong stay in Shanghai in the mid-1980s and many shorter return trips since.

Many parts of the book, however, rely on the important work that others have done on topics ranging from the massive rural-to-urban migration (the largest in human history) that has so radically transformed China's social landscape to the political legacy of Mao Zedong (Mao Tse-tung) (1893–1976).[2] In addition to articles and books by scholars, this volume relies heavily on the publications of a large coterie of very fine journalists and freelance writers who are contributing to what one scholar has aptly dubbed a "second Golden Age" of foreign writing about China.[3] These writers are providing stories and information to readers outside of China that challenge the stereotypes and oversimplifications that are so often buttressed by sound bite–driven reports and puffed-up punditry. The following chapters seek to contribute to this effort and to show some of the ways in which the West misunderstands China.

Two things to note in closing, each of which relates to the scope of this book. Although aimed at readers in all parts of the world, this book has inevitably been shaped by the fact that I am most familiar with the questions that Americans have about China, and the kinds of ideas and misconceptions that circulate within the United States. One chapter is, in fact, devoted exclusively to American misunderstandings of China, Chinese misunderstandings of the United States, and the things that the two countries, which often present themselves as completely unlike one another, have in common.

There are some advantages to reading a book on China that has an American tilt, such as this one. Both the United States and China have enormous economic clout and geopolitical significance. The two countries stand out in other ways: for example, the former is the largest per capita producer and the latter the largest overall producer of greenhouse-gas emissions. How people in these two countries view one another is arguably something everyone in the world needs to know.

Second, like other books in this series, this one does not strive to be encyclopedic, and many important issues will only be touched on. The three opening chapters, devoted to historical legacies, and the closing three chapters, which focus on contemporary dilemmas and future prospects, could easily be, and indeed have been, the focus of entire books. Still, I hope this work will provide a set of general frameworks so that the reader will come away with a clearer sense of a country that is, and will undoubtedly remain, a central player in many of the biggest stories of the 21st century.

MAP

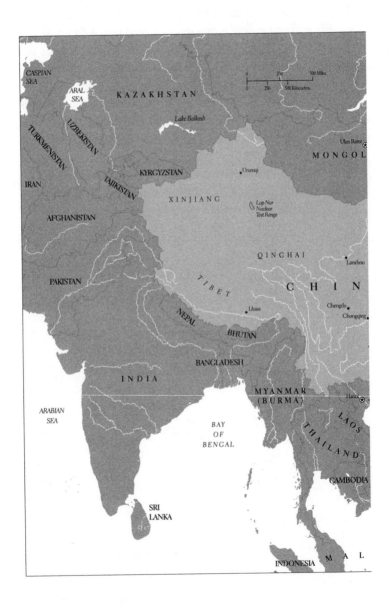

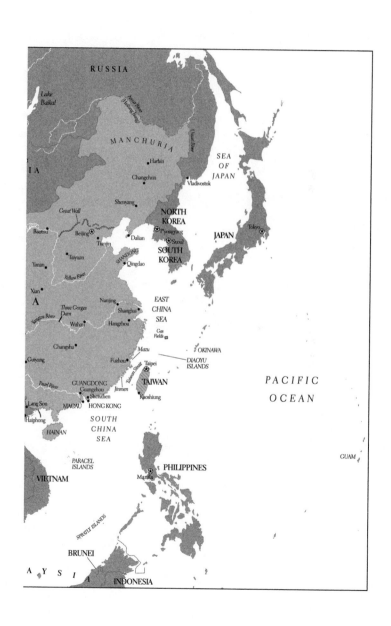

Part I

HISTORICAL LEGACIES

To understand today's China, it is crucial to know something about its past. And especially important for our purposes are those aspects of history that have direct relevance for contemporary developments, whether because of the precedent they set or because current leaders present themselves as breaking away from them or carrying them forward. With this in mind, and determined to avoid a wearying and confusing march through all the dynasties, the following three chapters offer up a selective (but I hope illuminating) quick run through the two millennia plus that get China from Confucius to Mao. The first chapter introduces major early Chinese schools of thought (especially the ideas of Confucius, since today's leaders seek to present today's China as a place where "Confucian" and Communist ideals complement one another). It also looks at the place that democratic traditions have had in China, showing that these are not just recent imports from the West. The second chapter focuses on political structures and major political ideas, including the concept of the "Mandate of Heaven," which legitimated imperial rule with reference to the interplay between spiritual and earthly dynamics. As well, it examines the similarities and differences between the ways that successive ruling houses (dynasties) governed China from the 3rd century B.C.E. until 1912, the year that China's last emperor abdicated and a republican form of government was established. Rounding out this first part of the book is a chapter on "Revolutions and Revolutionaries," which looks at the events and people who transformed the country during the period lasting from 1912 until Mao's death. It ends with a look at Mao's posthumous legacy, emphasizing the varied ways that the former leader has been seen and treated in the People's Republic of China (PRC) since his demise in 1976.

1

SCHOOLS OF THOUGHT

Who was Confucius?

Confucius (551 B.C.E.–479 B.C.E.) was a teacher and philosopher who lived during the Zhou (Chou) Dynasty (1045–256 B.C.E.), in what is known as the Spring and Autumn era (722 B.C.E.– 481 B.C.E.). As with those of his near contemporary Socrates, none of Confucius's writings have survived, and his views come down to us via a text produced after his death.[1] This is the *Analects*, which contains short statements attributed to Confucius (the origins of the "Confucius says" fortune cookie slips, though these were invented either in Japan in the 1800s or in California in the 1900s) and dialogues between the sage and his disciples.[2] The book covers a range of topics, from how a "true gentleman" behaves in his daily life (right down to how he eats with proper decorum) to how a ruler should govern (with a benevolent concern for the well-being of his subjects). One of its most famous statements, linked to both the high value placed on education in Chinese culture and the merito-cratic aspect of the Chinese political tradition, is that people are pretty much alike at birth but become differentiated via learning. Another well-known adage from the *Analects* says simply that it is a great pleasure to have friends come to visit from afar.

This adage gained new fame on August 8, 2008, when it was quoted at the start of the Beijing Games. The line, which was quoted again by a young man who put a question to President Obama during the Shanghai "town hall" meeting that was part of the American leader's November 2009 trip to China, had obvious relevance for the Olympic Opening Ceremony, since the live audience for the grand spectacle held in the Bird's Nest Stadium included foreign leaders, among them George W. Bush (the first sitting American president to attend the Olympics in a foreign country) and Russia's Vladimir Putin. Quoting Confucius also fit with the overall goal of the pageant and of Chinese Olympic publicity efforts generally, which was to demonstrate that the PRC has become a country that is open to the outside world and respectful of China's ancient as well as revolutionary traditions and values.

What were Confucius's core ideas?

The vision of morality sketched out in the Analects emphasizes the importance of three things: education, ritual, and relationships that are hierarchical yet provide benefits to both superior and inferior. Education was important because it was by studying the classical texts that a person could learn about and begin to emulate the actions of the most virtuous figures of past ages, including the legendary sages Yao and Shun (who lived long before the founding of the Zhou Dynasty) and figures such as the Duke of Zhou (who lived just a few centuries before Confucius). Ritual was important because it was a physical acting out of the best practices of earlier—and, to Confucius's way of thinking, purer—ages. And relationships in which there was a clear distinction between superior and inferior were valued, since in these the responsibilities of each side were clear.

What was his political vision?

Confucius saw political relationships as familial relationships writ large, meaning, for example, that rulers should behave toward those they governed the way that fathers should behave toward their children. He emphasized the importance of four relationships in particular, all of which he saw as reciprocal and all of which he thought involved analogous combinations of benevolence coming from one party and deference from the other. These relationships were those of ruler and minister, father and son, elder brother and younger brother, and husband and wife. (Later, followers of Confucius added a fifth relationship, more egalitarian than the others but never stressed as much: that between friend and friend.)

In each of the four main dyads discussed by Confucius, the former party was expected to protect the latter, and in return the latter was expected to be obedient to the former. The social order was threatened whenever people failed to act according to their prescribed roles.

Confucius lived in a time of civil wars and general instability, which continued during the Warring States era (475–221 B.C.E.) that followed soon after his death. He presented his views as providing a blueprint that, if followed by a just ruler, would guarantee that a state would have order within its own borders. He also promised that a ruler who adhered to his teachings would expand the reach of his state, since people living in other kingdoms would flock to live in such a peaceful, well-governed land.

How important was history to Confucius?

History was crucially important to Confucius. He claimed that a golden age of harmony had existed during the Western Zhou era (1046–770 B.C.E.), the time of the Duke of Zhou, the historical figure he admired most. Confucius called on people to study that age, which he lauded as a time when people knew their proper places within the social order.

According to the Analects, the first thing that a true king could do to improve the current age was to honor the past and revive the rituals and even the music of Western Zhou times, as a means to help all members of society rediscover proper deportment. This ruler should also ensure that his own behavior toward his subjects was a model of paternal benevolence at all moments, since this would lead to emulation by all others in a comparably superior position, so that a land with a good ruler would inevitably be one with good fathers (and other lineage elders) and good husbands.

There was a self-serving side to this argument. To accomplish these things, Confucius and his followers claimed, it would serve the true king well to rely upon advisers who were thoroughly versed in classical works and had made a specialty of studying the ways of the past. In other words, Confucius and his followers suggested that rulers heed the advice of scholarly specialists in ritual such as themselves.

Has Confucius always been venerated in China?

Confucius has not, in fact, always been venerated in China, but rather has had many ups and downs over the centuries. In some periods, his teachings have been ignored, though the notion that the best officials would be scholars and that education was important was prized throughout much of China's past, and in some eras, he has been despised.

You would not know this from the way he was treated during the Olympics. Not only did the Opening Ceremony begin with a quote from the Analects, but also a modern-day member of the Kong lineage that claims Confucius as an ancestor (the foreign term "Confucius" is derived from Kong Zi, or "Master Kong") played a symbolically important role in the pre-Games torch run. During the Opening Ceremony, three thousand performers dressed as the sage's disciples paraded through the Bird's Nest Stadium. This imagery was meant to suggest that for millennia (and presumably without interruption), Confucius has been a kind of national saint, a core symbol of China.

This notion would have seemed strange to many people living in China at various points in the past, including the early

1970s. Forty years ago, the odds would have seemed very long indeed that the day would ever come when Confucius would be accorded this place of honor in a national ceremony presided over by a head of the Chinese Communist Party.

At that point, late in the Maoist era (1949–1976), Confucius was excoriated in a mass campaign that presented him as a man whose hide-bound, anti-egalitarian ideas had done great harm to many generations of Chinese men and even more damage to many generations of Chinese women. He was blamed for having supported a wide range of unjust and immoral practices, from ancestor worship to viewing daughters as far less valuable than sons, which had kept China in a "feudal" state for millennia. And yet, in today's China, his views, albeit sometimes in modified form, are back in favor—so much so that in August 2008 television audiences throughout the country and around the world could see the then paramount leader of the Communist Party, President Hu Jintao (1942–), smiling down on those three thousand actors cast as Confucius's disciples, all of whom, incidentally, belonged to the performing troupes of the People's Liberation Army (PLA).

Had Confucius been an athlete and risen that quickly from has-been status to glory, Western television broadcasters would surely have dubbed him the "Comeback Kid" of the Beijing Games. As it was, the announcers tended to simply follow the script provided to them by the Xinhua (New China) News Agency and refer to the respectful treatment of Confucius as a natural expression of China's reverence for the traditions and great men of the country's past.

Was Confucius celebrated in his own times?

The sage was not particularly successful in gaining followers in his own lifetime. He would occasionally win the ear of a ruler, but he never had the opportunity he sought of being the long-term adviser of a major king. And things did not improve dramatically in the centuries immediately following his death, though important refinements of and additions to his thought were made during that time by figures such as Mencius (372–289 B.C.E.), second in importance only to Confucius in the development of what would later become known as Confucianism (the notion that their ideas constituted a clearly defined creed, comparable to a Western religion, was a much later invention).³ Up until the end of the Warring States period, in fact, Confucius's ideas were still but one school of thought, others being Daoism (Taoism), Legalism, and a host of now obscure creeds that were occasionally embraced by one or another ruler of the many competing kingdoms that made up what we now call "China." Even when Confucius's teachings took hold, it was often in a diluted form, combined with aspects of competing schools.

The proponents of some rival schools of thought, moreover, scoffed at Confucius and his beliefs. He was sometimes mocked by Daoists, who took a more egalitarian view of social relations than did the followers of Confucius and prized spontaneity over rituals, and by Legalists, who insisted that rulers should not strive to be admired for their virtues but rather take steps to ensure that they were respected and feared for the way they distributed rewards and punishments. The Daoists and Legalists, though disagreeing with one another on many things, agreed that the emphasis that Confucius put on the study of dusty classics was misguided. The former thought it wrong because the golden age they admired was the era of simplicity that preceded the creation of early Zhou Dynasty texts. The latter, a group of pragmatists, argued that rulers should adapt to the challenges of each new age.

As late as 221 B.C.E., when several of the embattled kingdoms of the Warring States were brought under the control of the head of the kingdom of Qin (Ch'in), it was still far from clear that Confucius would end up the most influential of early philosophers. The founder of the Qin Dynasty (221–206 B.C.E.), who became known to posterity as China's first emperor, had no time for Confucian ideas. He favored the Legalists, who told him how to maximize his authority, rather than the scholars, who told him how to behave benevolently. Qin Shi Huang, the first emperor, is now remembered (correctly) for the Terracotta Army built to serve him after death and (incorrectly) for creating the Great Wall. While he did build some large fortifications, the tourist sites one visits today and are often told date back to his time actually tend to be remnants of a much later wall-building dynasty, that of the Ming (1368–1644).[4] Yet the legend that Qin Shi Huang created the Great Wall is believable because the Legalist ideas he embraced enabled him to summon huge armies of laborers on demand.

The few historical accounts written near the lifetime of the first emperor, all crafted by historians serving the next dynasty, present Qin Shi Huang as a cruel despot.[5] In these works, he is described as providing a model of how not to rule, and as being someone who was so hated by his subjects that the dynasty he had dreamed would go on for centuries was overthrown by a popular rebellion that broke out soon after his death, just as his son's reign was beginning. As a result, while one can find traces of Legalist influence in the belief systems of many later dynasties, the creed was almost never officially endorsed after the Han Dynasty (206 B.C.E.–220 C.E.) was founded.

When did the ideas of Confucius gain influence?

It was not until the Qin Dynasty (whose name helped lead to China's being called "China," a term that sounds nothing like the primary Chinese terms for the country, such as "Zhongguo," meaning "Middle Kingdom") had fallen and the Han one was established that the ideas of Confucius became a core part of official ideology. And even then, Confucianism was combined with elements drawn from other schools of thought, such as Daoism and the Yin-Yang line of cosmological thinking (that emphasizes the interconnectedness of things that seem clearly different or even opposite), which was sometimes thought of as simply a part of the Daoist creed but was at other points viewed as its own school of thought.

Confucian ideals and practices were extolled by most successive dynasties, though they were often, as in the Han period, braided together with concepts and rituals taken from other creeds. These included Daoism (always a presence) and Chinese folk religious traditions. In addition, Confucianism was eventually influenced greatly by ideas associated with the imported but quickly domesticated belief system of Buddhism, which reached an early point of high influence in China during the Tang (T'ang) Dynasty (618–907), a cosmopolitan era when many ideas and objects flowed in through overland trade routes such as the Silk Road. Buddhist concepts were crucial in contributing to modifications within the Confucian tradition during the Song (Sung) Dynasty (960–1279) that were so great that the term "neo-Confucianism" is used to describe them.

How was Confucius viewed a century ago?

An important dip in Confucius's fortunes came in the early 1900s. Many Chinese intellectuals of the time argued that an attachment to "Confucian" values was responsible for the country's decline. They blamed Confucius for China's position of backwardness vis-à-vis the West and Japan, a formerly Confucian country that had begun to embrace European and American ways in the mid-19th century.

The most important pre-1949 anti-Confucian upsurge occurred during the New Culture movement (1915–1923). This was an iconoclastic struggle that one leader, Hu Shi (Hu Shih) (1891–1962), a student of the American philosopher John Dewey, would describe as "the Chinese Renaissance" in a book by that title based on lectures he gave in Chicago in the 1930s. The Chinese Renaissance also had things in common with the Enlightenment (its radical questioning of tradition and prizing of rationality) and the Western counterculture movement of the 1960s (its celebration of the value of youth, for example, and its celebration of new forms of art and literature).[6]

Participants in the New Culture movement, including a young Mao Zedong and the great Chinese writer Zhou Shuren (Chou Hsu-ren) (1881–1936), who published under the pen name Lu Xun (Lu Hsün), wrote scathingly about how Confucius had shaped a China in which age was venerated at the expense of youth, women were repressed, individualism and creativity were stifled, and a cult of tradition prevented innovation. To join the modern world, they argued, China needed to jettison Confucius and everything that he represented, embracing the best that the West had to offer as, they claimed, Japan had done—resulting in its rising in global influence. They also insisted that intellectuals stop using classical Chinese, which was far removed from vernacular forms of communication, and develop a "plain speech" (baihua) form of writing to take its place.

Some, but not all, New Culture veterans would stick to anti-Confucian positions for decades. Others, though, would eventually abandon these, after throwing their lot in with the Nationalist Party, which began as a culturally radical group but later became a culturally conservative organization.

The Nationalists of the 1930s, under the leadership of Chiang Kai-shek (1887–1975), would, in fact, be responsible for a major Confucian revival. Chiang insisted that China's best route forward was to find a way to combine Confucian values with the most advanced technologies available in and best ideas coming from Japan and the West. Despite being a Christian, Chiang elevated the Chinese sage's birthday to the status of a state holiday. He argued that the emphasis on tradition, family, social order, and clearly delineated hierarchies in Confucianism could go hand in hand with the teachings of the Bible.

Is Confucianism a religion?

Confucius himself was more of a philosopher than a religious figure. Even though his emphasis on looking up to elders fit in well with the practices of ancestor worship, which predated his time and remained a mainstay of Chinese rural and sometimes also court life for many centuries after his death, he claimed that it was so hard to understand the affairs of human beings that he was in no position to speculate about the details of the afterlife.

Nevertheless, throughout history, he has occasionally been elevated to the status of a saint or a godlike figure, with temples being devoted to him (including some that have recently been spruced up by the regime) and his hometown of Qufu being transformed into a pilgrimage site (with, lately, a bit of a theme-park aspect thrown in). Ironically, the period of rule by the Christian Chiang Kai-shek was a time in which Confucius was revered, as, even more ironically, is the current era of rule by the allegedly still atheist Communist Party.

Foreigners have often looked at China and said that the country has three major religions: Confucianism, Daoism, and Buddhism. Though Confucianism is more a philosophy than a religion, Daoism and Buddhism are indeed important systems of thought in China. Yet religious identity is also far more fluid than in the Judeo-Christian West, as many Chinese will move among the three depending on context. Someone, for example, might worship at a Confucian temple right before an important school exam (due to Confucius's association with learning) but also consider him- or herself a practicing Buddhist, adhering to a vegetarian diet and reciting sutras every morning. Buddhism, like all other religions, was suppressed during the Mao era, but it has enjoyed a popular revival in recent decades. Like Confucian temples, many Buddhist ones have also recently been renovated and, sometimes, turned into tourist destinations where people can observe "releasing life" ceremonies (live fish and birds are released into the wild), walk through a restored temple complex, have lunch at a vegetarian restaurant, and finish their visit with a trip to the gift shop.

How did Confucius fare after 1949?

Not surprisingly, when the Communist Party took power on October 1, 1949, after driving Chiang into exile on Taiwan, the birthday of Confucius immediately ceased being celebrated. The anti-Confucius campaign of the early 1970s was just the most radical and focused expression of an anti-Confucian viewpoint that predominated throughout the Mao years and that continued during the brief post-Mao period, when China's paramount leader was Hua Guofeng (Hua Kuo-feng) (1921–2008), a kind of place-holder authority figure who was soon edged out of the top spot by Deng Xiaoping (Teng Hsiao-p'ing) (1904–1997) and spent the last decades of his life holding only relatively minor official posts.

The first decades of Communist rule were, moreover, a time when, contrary to Confucian ideals, egalitarian values were celebrated—though new forms of inequality took root, with cadres emerging as a class with special privileges. During this period, the government worked to minimize the importance of the family as a social unit by creating new communal units, such as collectives and communes. It was a time when China's leadership stressed adaptation to present conditions and creating a new future rather than celebrating any past golden age. It was also one of those rare times in Chinese history when Legalism was sometimes viewed in a positive way. This is because Mao, in typically iconoclastic fashion, sometimes said that when it came to China's various imperial rulers, the first emperor, with his Legalist ideas, disdain for book-learning detached from pragmatic concerns, and ability to get big things done, was among the best.

Why is Confucius back in favor?

The renewal of official veneration of Confucius, though representing an about-face for the Communist Party, is not that hard to understand. It fits in with a general tendency by the current regime to emphasize continuity with the past. Official statements are full of references to the country's glorious "5,000 years" of "unbroken" cultural development and references to China being the "only unified and continuous civilization" that still has a presence in the modern world.[7] This assertion is a problematic one, given how many changes over time there have been in the size and shape of China as a country and the values and traditions of the people living within its borders. Nevertheless, a mix-and-match approach to the past is now the order of the day, in which anything that suggests past greatness is held up as worthy of respect.

The image of China's present as carrying forward elements of its distant past is actively fostered via positive references to and celebrations of not just Confucius but also other people who lived during ancient times and symbols linked to very early periods of history. This is true even of sites that were seen as reminders of the failings rather than the glories of the past as recently as Mao's time. For example, Mao did not treat the Forbidden City as sacred. He was happy to allow the home of the emperors of China's last two dynasties, the Ming and the Qing (Ch'ing) (1644–1911), fall into disrepair, and during the Mao years, the grounds sometimes contained sculptures that drew attention to the unjust ways that ordinary Chinese were treated by rulers and landlords in the dark period that came before the Communist Revolution. Now, however, the old palace complex has been carefully restored and is presented as a symbol of the glamour and beauty—not decadence—of the past. The Forbidden City is a site that visiting dignitaries are supposed to tour, as President Obama did on his first trip to China in 2009, and view as representing the glories of the country's artistic and architectural traditions.

It is also telling that the old pattern of feeling a need to choose between celebrating the words of Confucius or the deeds of the first emperor has been abandoned. The Analects and the Terracotta Warriors are now treated as complementary symbols of an ancient China that achieved great things in many realms.

This promiscuous pairing of ancient icons often thought to represent contrasting traditions fits in with the desire of China's current leaders to cultivate national pride by presenting the country as one that was great in the past and has become great again on their watch. This is partly because it is in the regime's interest for people of Chinese descent in Taiwan, Australia, the United States, and other parts of the world (even those with no love for Communism) to identify with, travel to, and invest in the PRC.

There is also a more specific reason that Confucius is back. This is because there is a good fit between the emphasis that Confucius and his followers have always placed on social harmony and the focus that Hu Jintao and other current Chinese leaders have placed on stability.

Mao, in keeping with Marxist tradition, stressed that progress is made via conflict and struggle. By contrast, though China's current leaders claim to still adhere to Marxism, there are strong—and intentional—Confucian resonances to the slogans championing cooperation in creating a "harmonious society" (hexie shehui) that have become identified with Hu.

There was even a moment during the Olympics Opening Ceremony when the contours of this catchphrase's main character, "he" (harmony), were visually displayed in an eye-catching manner. And the list of fifty officially approved slogans for the large parade held on October 1, 2009, to mark the sixtieth birthday of the PRC included several with "hexie," one of which called on the people to help the party "build a socialist harmonious society and promote social equity and justice."

How exactly has the regime used Confucius in recent years?

In addition to sanctioning the sage's appearance during the Olympics and echoing the Analects and later Confucian texts in calls for "harmonious" social relations, since 2004, the Chinese government has sponsored the creation and funding of "Confucius Institutes" in many parts of the world. These are modeled in part on the German Goethe Institutes, and their stated intent is simply to further understanding of China's cultural legacy via things such as offering classes in the Chinese language and courses on Chinese history that emphasize continuities with the past and the "5,000 years of Chinese civilization" idea. One key contrast with the Goethe Institutes and other comparable undertakings, though, is that, as Lionel Jensen stresses in a careful look at the topic, unlike their more independent German counterparts, Confucius Institutes are "largely underwritten by and must report to the Chinese government."[8]

In the West, controversy has sometimes followed these Confucius Institutes. In the most extreme cases, commentators have suggested that they are part of a Chinese Communist plot to infiltrate American communities. Pointing to the fact that the money and personnel to staff the institutes come from a ministry within the PRC government, such alarmism hearkens back to the "Red Scare" of the 1950s. There is also, though, a much more sensible basis for concern. Namely, some scholars worry that a university that has funding coming from an arm of the Beijing government could end up curtailing intellectual freedom on campus, perhaps in subtle ways. The Chinese authorities have used many kinds of pressure—for example, to try to get officials around the world to refrain from meeting publicly with the Dalai Lama—so it is easy to imagine veiled or overt threats of a removal of Confucius Institute funds from an organization that sponsored a talk by him. Sometimes, representatives of the Chinese government are invited to attend campus speaker series supported by Confucius Institutes, so it is also possible that organizers of these series might steer clear of inviting foreign scholars with particularly close ties to dissidents in exile or mainland political prisoners to be part of these events, simply to minimize the chance for any awkwardness on the part of a patron.[9]

What is too rarely noted in commentaries on these Confucius Institutes is that, given the anti-Confucius stance of the Chinese Communist Party under Mao, Beijing's choice of nomenclature is shocking to those with a sense of history. It is as though, late in the history of the Soviet Union, Moscow had set up "Tsar Nicholas Institutes" to spread understanding of Russian culture around the world.

The revival of official Confucianism, which has led to the restoration of temples devoted to Confucius and the erection of statues of the sage (in some parts of China, these now outnumber the ones of Mao left over from the days when those proliferated), is one of many echoes in today's China of the era of Chiang Kai-shek. Now, as then, the leader of a party that had previously been associated with upheaval (the Nationalist one also began as a radical revolutionary organization) is drawing inspiration from a philosopher who championed tradition and harmony.

There has also been a popular revival of interest in Confucius. One of the best-selling nonfiction books published in the PRC this century has been a work on the Analects by the academic-turned-media-personality Yu Dan. Her book, a kind of *Chicken Soup for the Soul* with Chinese characteristics that has sold millions of copies and has also appeared in English, has been criticized for bowdlerizing the ideas of Confucius. But there is no question that it has proved very popular.[10]

The government has hailed the Yu Dan phenomenon as evidence of the complementary nature of the people's and the regime's longing for social harmony. One could, though, also see it as part of a broader hunger among disillusioned people for something new to believe in—even if that something new is merely something very old repackaged in a novel way.

Yet the PRC regime has subtly scaled back its sponsorship of Confucius since the Olympics. One of the oddest incidents involving the sage occurred in 2011, when a thirty-one-foot-tall statue of Confucius was installed in Tiananmen Square, China's most symbolically fraught public space, that January. In April, however, the massive statue disappeared overnight. It had been moved to a courtyard within the National Museum, just off the square. While government leaders claimed this had always been their plan for the statue, the sudden and covert nature of the move raised eyebrows among those who scrutinize the regime's actions to see which way the political wind is blowing.[11] Although the Chinese leadership continues to emphasize Confucius and the need to develop a harmonious society, the state revival of Confucianism is not as intense now as it was around 2008.

Did Confucianism hinder imperial China's economic development?

The influential German social theorist Max Weber certainly thought Confucianism hindered imperial China's economic development. According to Weber, while Protestantism encouraged the sort of innovation and concern with transformation that drives capitalism, the emphasis Confucius put on recapturing the glories of past times was a brake on development. In addition, Confucian texts often claimed that, aside from the ruling family, there were four basic social groups in China; the two most valuable ones in the eyes of Confucius and his followers were scholars (who made sure that the country was well governed) and farmers (who provided society with food); of lesser value were artisans (who were not essential but made products that were useful); and least valued of all, indeed despised, were the merchants (who did not contribute to the good of the community at all).

There are two problems, however, with thinking of Confucianism as a block on economic development.

First, as work by Kenneth Pomeranz has shown, as late as 1750, the most economically vibrant parts of Confucian China were roughly as commercialized and prosperous as the most economically vibrant parts of Protestant Europe. Factors other than modes of thought thus need to be seen as leading to what Pomeranz calls the "great divergence" between Western and Chinese economic development after that point.[12] Other things that made a difference, Pomeranz claims, included the distribution of natural resources (England was lucky to have large coal supplies located in parts of the country that were close to its commercial centers, for example) and the various forms that imperialism took, with European empires expanding overseas, whereas the Qing just moved inland. Britain's extraordinary takeoff, he insists, had much to do with the fact that it could make use of land-intensive products from overseas, facilitated by the legacies of slavery and colonialism and compensating for Europe's relatively low agricultural yields per acre, and had domestic coal deposits that were relatively easy to access. The Qing had plenty of areas to mine, but they were in regions that were hard to reach before the era of railroads.

The second problem with the idea that Confucianism and advanced economic development cannot go hand in hand is that many of the economic success stories of recent decades have involved East Asian countries that, like China, were influenced greatly by Confucianism. After the rapid takeoff of Japan, Hong Kong, South Korea, Singapore, and Taiwan, the notion that Confucian values stand in the way of capitalism seems untenable.

There is also the fact that today's China, while not exactly capitalist—some 70 percent of the top five hundred companies in the PRC are state owned and much of its overall wealth is in the form of government assets—has experienced a great economic boom. That this transpired in an era of renewed celebration of Confucius is another nail in the Weberian conceptual coffin.

In the wake of recent economic shifts, some people have turned Weber upside down and claimed that, while Confucian thinkers may have dismissed merchants as unproductive, the kind of family-centered and generally collectivist and cooperative approach to life fostered by Confucianism is conducive to certain forms of highly profitable business activities. Whether or not this is true, the idea that people who share "Confucian" values, however defined, are naturally well disposed to do business with one another definitely matters. The largest investors in joint enterprises with the Chinese state have tended to be companies based in neighboring countries, including Taiwan, that see themselves as sharing a cultural bond, partly via Confucius, with the PRC.

Does China have an indigenous "democratic" tradition?

Chinese modes of thought are sometimes described as particularly well suited to authoritarianism, and the emphasis on hierarchy and deference within Confucianism and on harsh punishments within Legalism lend credence to this notion. And yet, there are also some elements of the multistranded intellectual tradition of China that are more democratic than authoritarian.

For example, as already noted, Daoist classics encourage people to view hierarchical relationships with skepticism and question whether those in positions of superiority are any better than or different from anyone else. This is not a "democratic" notion in the specific sense of suggesting that elections be held to determine who should lead a country, but it is a viewpoint that provides a basis for challenging rather than accepting power relations within a society.

In addition, even within the Confucian tradition, there is a democratic strand. This is linked to the concept, not exclusively Confucian but certainly associated with Confucianism, of the "Mandate of Heaven" (*Tianming*) as the basis for political authority. The idea here is that emperors were the earthly representation of Heaven (*Tian*), a depersonalized spiritual force whose role in running the universe was comparable to that of the emperor's role on earth (literally, *Tianxia*, or "the realm of all under Heaven").

Heaven offered a mandate (*ming*) to each new dynasty, according to this view, but this right to govern was revocable. If an emperor failed to carry out his role correctly, Heaven could transfer the mandate to a new ruler.

Mencius provided the most elaborate early vision of the workings of this process. He claimed that rulers deserved to govern only as long as they demonstrated a true affection for the people and protected their interests. This complemented the emphasis in the Analects on the ruler being like a "father" to his subjects. Mencius went so far as to claim that rulers who failed to behave benevolently toward those below them in the social order forfeited their right to be treated deferentially.

In one famous formulation, he stated that while rulers govern "by the will of Heaven, Heaven hears with the ears and sees with the eyes of the people." This meant that if the people, with good cause, were thoroughly dissatisfied, Heaven would naturally find it suitable to stop protecting the emperor and would add its support to those seeking to establish a new dynasty. In such a case, rebellion was both likely and morally justified.

This is, again, not an argument for elections, which those of us living in the West and some other countries (India, for example) tend to equate with democracy. Still, it is an important expression of a kind of democratic sentiment.

What is the Chinese term for democracy and what exactly does it mean?

The standard Chinese term for "democracy" is *"minzhu,"* which, like many complex concepts, is composed of two characters with separate meanings. *"Min"* means "people," while *"zhu"* means "rule."

This compound word, like the original Greek term for democracy (which has a parallel etymology tied to "people" and "rule"), can be interpreted in various ways. It can conjure images of direct rule by the masses or imply simply that the best government is led by a ruler who pays great attention to the interests of the population at large. There is another interpretation of *minzhu* that has long been popular among some highly educated Chinese. This might be called representative democracy sans elections; the idea is that intellectuals should advise rulers to ensure that the interests of the people are respected.

One basis for this idea, which is linked to the emphasis Confucius put on learning, is that, from Han times onward, civil service examinations were used to fill many government positions. The use of tests that required mastery of Confucian precepts for those seeking high office became particularly important after the expansion of the system during the Song Dynasty. By no means did emperors always take the counsel of intellectuals, but the idea that intellectuals are natural spokespeople for the masses took root and has endured.

If the government's promotion of Confucianism represents one kind of reworking of an old idea to further a 21st-century mission, then efforts by critical intellectuals to present the current regime as morally bankrupt and to call for change in the name of the people represents another. Both proponents of the current order and those fighting to change the way China is governed can tap into elements of the country's multistranded intellectual and political traditions.

2

IMPERIAL CHINA

What were the main early dynasties?

A standard way to break up Chinese history is to start with 221 B.C.E., the year that Qin Shi Huang transformed various small states into something big enough to qualify as an empire. There were earlier dynasties ruling part or all of the land just north and just south of the Yellow River, which make up the heartland of what we now call "China" and where many Chinese capital cities, including the present one, Beijing, have stood.

The earliest of these ancient dynasties was the Xia (Hsia) (2070–1600 B.C.E.), often viewed as a mythic entity, since there is little reliable evidence to show that it even existed. Next came the Shang (1760?–1122? B.C.E.), whose rituals of state included the use of oracle bones (animal parts used for divination), some of which have been unearthed. These contain writing that can be linked to the characters that were used in classical texts and then eventually became the building blocks of modern Chinese. Following this came the Zhou (1046–256 B.C.E.), whose early years in power Confucius extolled as a perfect time. None of these dynasties controlled nearly as great a territory as the Qin.[1]

The leader of the rebellion that toppled the Qin became the first emperor of the Han Dynasty, which would transform China into a much larger country and, as we have seen, would be the first to give the ideas of Confucius a central part in state ideology. The Han period of rule and expansion was roughly contemporaneous with and similar in some basic ways to the Roman age in the West.

The Han grand historian Sima Qian (Ssu-Ma Ch'ien) (c. 145 or 135–86 B.C.E.), China's first great writer of history and someone often still considered the preeminent Chinese chronicler, repudiated the activities of the Qin. Nevertheless, in the first of many ironic continuities of this kind, the Han left in place basic elements of the political system that China's first emperor had created, including the use of a civil bureaucracy differentiated from the military, a key Qin innovation. One indication of just how important the Han period was is that, while the term "Qin" helped provide a name for the country, the name of the following dynasty was taken as the name for the land's inhabitants. The majority population of the PRC is dubbed the "Han," and official statistical counts place nine out of ten citizens of the country in this broadly defined ethnic group.

How did dynasties rule?

One enduring feature of the Chinese imperial system was the special status of the emperor as both religious and political figure, a man who performed ritual functions as an intermediary between Tian (Heaven) and the human world. Another enduring feature was the central political role played not just by the monarch but also by members of his family (and, rarely, her family; with only a couple of exceptions, the ruler of imperial China was a man).

In China's imperial system, in contrast to many other monarchical ones, the successor to the emperor was not necessarily his eldest son. As a result, intense political maneuvering before and immediately after a ruler's death was common.

In addition, since the emperor often had children with more than one wife and one or more concubines, the stakes of succession were great for many people. And there were many mothers, uncles, aunts, and so forth of a monarch or monarch-to-be who could wield influence, especially since close family members were sometimes appointed regents of young successors to the Dragon Throne.

The most powerful people in imperial China, other than members of the ruling family, tended to be either scholar-officials or eunuchs. The former group included ministers of state, provincial governors, and the crucially important local magistrates, who fulfilled at the local level a comparable mixture of ritual and political roles to those the emperor performed for the entire empire.

Having only eunuchs as palace servants and banning men capable of impregnating royal wives and concubines from living in the palace ensured order within the imperial household; thus, in this realm, the potential for disputes over the paternity of potential heirs was minimized. The highest-ranking bureaucrats were always supposed to be more powerful than any eunuch, but due to their special access to the emperor and other members of the royal family, eunuchs sometimes had the greatest influence. When dynasties were criticized for becoming corrupt, eunuchs were often blamed—though in a misogynist vein, imperial decline was also sometimes attributed to the nefarious behind-the-scenes workings of palace women, from mothers of young emperors to the scheming concubines of elderly male rulers.[2]

What was the "dynastic cycle"?

The concept of the "dynastic cycle" held that one dynasty should periodically give way to another. The founders of dynasties (whether rebels who succeeded or the leaders of foreign armies who seized the country) could come to power, according to this line of thought, only because Heaven saw them as virtuous and deserving to rule. Over time, however, their descendants were likely to become less mindful of the people's needs, a variation on the Western adage that power corrupts. The political order would then need to be purified through transfer of the mandate to a new group. This would restart the cycle of virtuous founder and decadent descendants.

Because the natural and the political worlds were viewed as analogous to and in sync with one another, indications that the Mandate of Heaven had been lost by the current leader and was ready to be claimed by a new one included unusual events, such as natural disasters. Eclipses could also be interpreted as signals of Heaven's displeasure about some occurrence in the human world. Emperors therefore wanted to know when these would occur, in order to be prepared to offer the people a suitable interpretation of the event.

What were the political implications of this cyclical view?

In contrast to monarchical orders in which every new ruler can trace descent to a common ancestor (e.g., the current Japanese emperor claims to be part of the same lineage as the first one), an order in which there were occasional shifts in rulers was assumed to be a good thing.

Bureaucrats and ministers (who generally attained their posts by passing exams rather than by inheriting their positions à la European aristocrats) faced a tough choice whenever rebellions started or foreign armies threatened the state. They had to decide whether the current ruling house had lost the Mandate of Heaven or not, and whether, in guarding the interests of the people, they should or should not switch sides.

Finally, since new dynasties often maintained their predecessors' institutions, there was considerable continuity. A new dynasty often relied heavily upon officials who had served the previous dynasty and then jumped ship to join the new one.

Were all dynasties the same?

Despite the continuities listed so far, there were always important variations among dynasties, with each leaving its distinct mark. One basic difference among dynasties is that they governed territories of radically varying sizes. A map of today's PRC shows borders defining "China" that came into being only after the Qing Dynasty had engaged in many decades of imperial expansion after taking power in 1644.

Even some very significant dynasties governed territories much smaller than this. Consider, for instance, that the Song (960–1279), who ruled a land mass much less than half the size of the PRC, not only oversaw the institutionalization of the civil service system but also governed during a period of rapid economic development so dramatic that some scholars locate the start of "modern" China in that period.

The Ming Dynasty (1368–1644) had a larger domain than that of the Song. But Ming emperors controlled neither Tibet, the mountainous region far west of the Yellow River heartland that the PRC claims has been part of China for many centuries, nor Xinjiang, the region in the northwestern corner of the PRC whose name (the characters for it mean "New Frontier") refers to its late incorporation into the Chinese empire (during Qing times).

Just as there were dynasties that sometimes failed to govern lands that are now considered part of China, there were also emperors who ruled territory that is no longer part of the PRC. Vietnam, for instance, was sometimes but not always part of the Chinese empire before the 20th century, and there were periods when parts of it were or were not under the control of China's emperor.

In addition, dynasties that came to power via wars of conquest took on the roles of the rulers they displaced but always modified the system they inherited. This was especially true of dynasties that had their ethnic and cultural roots on the steppes of Central and Northeastern Asia, in regions such as Mongolia and Manchuria that were to the north of and less agricultural than the Chinese heartland.

Under Kublai Khan and other rulers of the Yuan Dynasty (1271–1368), for example, Confucian exams were suspended.

And the early Manchu emperors of the Qing wrote some documents in their native language and some documents in Chinese.

The Qing set up a dual-track official system in which some posts were reserved for ethnic Manchus, while others were given to members of the Han ethnic group, to which the majority of people living south of the Great Wall belonged. The Qing also maintained special troops (the "Banner forces"), composed only of people who traced their descent to the northern steppes.

How did dynasties interact with foreign countries?

One shared characteristic of most dynasties was a view that the land the emperor governed was of central importance. Chinese emperors, like the heads of many other empires, tended to think of their domain as the most important in the immediate region, perhaps even in the entire world. Partly because Confucian thought emphasized clear hierarchies, the emperors expected heads of other states to treat them with deference, in return offering these entities protection and benevolence.

Nevertheless, the way that individual dynasties and indeed individual emperors dealt with the outside world varied. Some rulers were much more open to and involved in international trade and exploration than were others. There were Ming emperors, for example, who welcomed Jesuits from Europe, partly because Western advances in astronomy were helpful in predicting eclipses. It was also a Ming emperor who funded the fabled naval expeditions of Zheng He (Cheng Ho) (1371–1433), who most reputable scholars are convinced did not "discover America" (as a 2003 best-seller would have it) but did guide a fleet that probably made it as far as Africa.[3]

Other rulers were suspicious of outsiders and took a more restrictive stance toward international connections. They were convinced that increased contact with foreigners was unnecessary and perhaps dangerous.

Most notably, in the late 1700s, the Qing decided to limit Western traders' and missionaries' access to China. Chinese trade with Southeast Asia was robust and operated through many ports, but Westerners eager to exploit new markets for their goods and find new souls to convert were allowed to drop anchor at only one southern city, Guangzhou (Canton). The only exception to this rule concerned the Portuguese, who had a beachhead of their own in Macao, a city near Guangzhou that had been ceded to them as a colony.

What was the Opium War?

The policy of prohibiting foreign ships from anchoring in most Chinese ports was a source of discontent for Westerners who dreamed, as their counterparts of both earlier and more recent times have, of finding in China's heartland an endless supply of customers and converts. They did not believe the Qing line that China was a self-sufficient empire capable of producing all that its people required and that, hence, the West had nothing of great value to offer.

The frustration of Western traders and missionaries grew in the early 1800s as the British desire for (and indeed dependence on) tea produced in China grew. Since European and American merchants had failed to find any product that the Chinese wanted to buy in comparably significant quantities, a trade imbalance favoring China developed, leading to the flow of silver out of the West and into the Qing Empire.

To counteract this, and to take advantage of easy access to the high-quality poppies grown in India, which had become a British colony, traders from Britain began to market opium in China (with American merchants, who often got their poppies from Turkey, following suit). These traders hoped that opium would prove as addictive for the Chinese as tea had proven for Londoners.

The Qing introduced strict laws against buying and selling opium, but the foreign strategy proved effective, and a trade imbalance favoring the West developed. Western traders were always finding new ways to get the drug into China (thanks to help from Chinese smugglers, in many cases), and demand for the narcotic in China consistently grew, particularly in areas near Guangzhou.

Tensions mounted, with each side claiming the moral high ground. The Westerners insisted that free trade was a God-given right that the Qing were barbarically denying them, and they argued that if only they were granted free access to all Chinese ports, they would find markets for goods other than opium. Qing officials, meanwhile, decried the Westerners for the villainy of flouting local laws and bringing a dangerous substance into the country.

War broke out in 1839, and Qing forces quickly suffered a series of military defeats. In order to stop the Western iron ships from heading toward the Chinese capital, the Qing signed a treaty very favorable to the foreigners.

What impact did the Opium War have?

The war had devastating effects: economically, it had been costly; politically, it raised doubts among some as to whether the dynasty had a firm hold on the Mandate of Heaven; and psychologically, the war undermined the longstanding notion that China was the most advanced and powerful country in the world.[4]

As part of the Treaty of Nanjing signed at the conclusion of hostilities, Britain gained partial control over Hong Kong, which it held as a Crown colony (and, later, a British-dependent territory) until returning it to China in 1997. (Full British control over Hong Kong was accomplished in stages throughout the 19th century, concluding in 1898.) Britain also secured the right for its merchants and missionaries to set up self-governing settlements in several other coastal cities, dubbed "treaty ports," including Shanghai; and the French and Americans, and later the Japanese, used force and the threat of force to ensure that the same privileges were extended to their nationals.

Why did the Qing Dynasty fall?

Until the 1970s, scholars often viewed the Qing as having had a firm hold on the country until the Opium War. The story of the first two centuries of Qing rule was presented as characterized largely by triumphs, with strong and long-reigning emperors extending the reach of the empire into Central Asia. In this narrative, the mid-19th-century clashes with the West marked the beginning of the end of a dynasty that had been in good shape. Now, historians have begun to appreciate that there were realms other than that of foreign affairs that strained Qing rule.

What internal developments weakened the Qing?

One source of strain on the Qing was demographic: the population of China grew tremendously in the late 1700s and early to mid-1800s, at least doubling (perhaps tripling or quadrupling) in a century. This placed a great deal of pressure on the country simply because there were more mouths to feed.

It also caused problems for the Qing because the number of magistrates did not increase. This meant that, by 1830, each of these multitasking bureaucrats (responsible for presiding over trials, collecting taxes, maintaining granaries, and officiating at local rituals) was overseeing many more people than ever before.

What was the significance of peasant rebellions?

The Qing also faced a problem of popular rebellions. These took many forms, ranging from piracy and banditry to religiously inflected insurrections led by prophets who called on the faithful to rise up. Notable revolts included an uprising led by the Eight Trigrams sect in 1813, which was quickly suppressed, but at the cost of some 70,000 lives. Another was a holy war launched in the 1820s and the 1830s by the Central Asian leader Jahangir, who sought to free Xinjiang from imperial control.[5]

The White Lotus Rebellion that convulsed much of the Chinese heartland from 1796 until 1804 was even more significant. This revolt was linked to Maitreyan Buddhism, a form of the originally Indian religion that was particularly popular in parts of China and Southeast Asia. The White Lotus Rebellion had a millenarian aspect to it; that is, its followers believed that a new age was about to begin and that those adhering to the faith would fare well in the coming order. Leaders of Chinese Buddhist sects often discouraged outright rebellion, encouraging their followers to wait quietly for change to come. But at some points they called for direct action, and these calls found especially receptive ears among people struggling with natural disasters such as droughts and floods or angered by what they viewed as excessive taxation.[6]

The White Lotus Rebellion, which began with tax protests in a poor mountainous area, was a classic example of a call for action that resonated within an economically desperate population. A potent addition to the mix was anti-Manchu sentiment and Han chauvinism—that is, a belief that control of China should be returned to members of the main Chinese ethnic group. For some participants, a key attraction of the movement was the belief that it would lead to the restoration of the Ming, the ethnically Chinese dynasty that had preceded the Qing.

The dynasty suppressed the rebellion, but at a great cost. According to a leading historian of Chinese religious movements, the Qing spent "the rough equivalent of five years' revenue (200 million ounces of silver)" on military campaigns against the rebels, and their troops were defeated in enough battles that the "Manchu banner forces' reputation for invincibility" was permanently lost.[7] When the Opium War broke out, the Qing Dynasty was already reeling from a series of major challenges, contending with both novel issues and popular rebellions of the sort that had toppled previous dynasties.

What was the Taiping Uprising?

The Taiping Uprising was a millenarian insurrection of enormous proportions that is probably the most important 19th-century event whose name is still not a household word in the West.

The Qing Dynasty was forced to contend with nearly continuous domestic revolts and additional international conflicts from the 1840s through the 1890s. The most devastating revolt of this period was the Taiping Uprising (1848–1864), a massive and bloody insurrection whose death toll far exceeded that of the nearly contemporaneous American Civil War.

The movement's leader was Hong Xiuquan, a frustrated scholar who had had a breakdown after failing the civil service exams multiple times and suffered hallucinations that imbued him with a sense of divine purpose and seem to have been shaped by things he had read in a missionary tract years before. His visions convinced him that he was Christ's younger brother and was destined to expel the Manchus (whom he came to think of as demonic figures and decried as members of a bestial race) from China and transform it into a Christian land. His particular version of Christianity was so outlandish to most foreigners that, while he initially gained some Western support, international forces ended up siding with the Qing against him.

At the height of the struggle, the fiercely anti-Confucian Hong (after failing the exams, he had no fondness for the sage) governed a territory roughly the size of France. He behaved in many ways like the founder of a new dynasty, even instituting a civil service examination system—with the novel twist that candidates had to demonstrate mastery over his idiosyncratic interpretation of biblical teachings rather than Confucian classics and famous commentaries on those classics, the main staple of Qing official exams.

Why was the 1894–1895 Sino–Japanese War so important?

The Qing fought further wars with European powers after 1842, including one that ended in 1860 with foreign troops destroying one of the dynasty's most elaborate palaces, Yuanmingyuan, but the most significant international conflict of the second half of the 19th century was a war with Japan concerning which country would control Korea. That war began in 1894 and ended a year later with another defeat for the Qing. The Opium War had undermined the notion that the Qing governed the world's most powerful empire; this latest war demonstrated that it was no longer even the dominant regional power in East Asia.

This defeat led some intellectuals to call for the dynasty to embrace the kind of widespread adaptation of Western ideas and institutions that were credited with strengthening Japan, and they gained the ear of a reform-minded emperor. The result was a bold but short-lived effort to radically reshape China's political and educational institutions, which was known as the "100 Days Reform" of 1898. Conservatives within the dynasty fought back, however, and the emperor was placed under house arrest, though some institutions established by the reformers remained, such as the school that evolved into today's Peking University, China's most prestigious college.

The conservative faction, whose supporters included not just members of the ruling family but also some diehard Confucian scholars (though there were reformers who creatively proposed that Confucius would have approved of their reforms), argued that the West and Japan might have superior armed forces but that Chinese institutions were better, since they were rooted in superior values.

What was the Boxer Rebellion?

The Boxer Rebellion (1899–1901) is greatly misunderstood outside of China. It began with bands of young men attacking Chinese Christians and foreign missionaries in North China. It took on new dimensions in the summer of 1900, when these insurgents held Western and Japanese residents of Beijing hostage for fifty-five days, and the Qing Dynasty, which had vacillated between viewing the insurgents as bandits to be suppressed and loyalists to be praised, threw their support behind the Boxers. An international force of soldiers marching under eight flags lifted the siege.

The crisis continued well into 1901, as foreign soldiers carried out campaigns of retribution and members of the Qing ruling family fled the capital. It ended in September 1901, when the Qing Dynasty, which had been allowed to return to Beijing after a brief period of exile in the north, signed a treaty, known as the Boxer Protocol. This accord included a stipulation that a giant indemnity be paid to compensate for the loss of foreign lives and property, with no comparable recompense for Chinese suffering at the hands of invading armies.

Another key part of the protocol was designed to justify the continuation of Qing rule. The foreign powers had decided that, for all their complaints about the Qing, they preferred the dynastic devil they knew to any alternative. As a result, as part of the settlement of the crisis, both sides agreed to promote the fiction that the Boxers had been anti-dynastic "rebels," rather than members of a loyalist insurrection that had at times achieved official support.

How has this crisis been misunderstood?

Western misunderstandings of the Boxer Rebellion begin with the use of misleading nomenclature. It was not really a "rebellion," for the insurgents often expressed a desire to support the Qing. The motivation for the uprising was not anger at the dynasty but a desire to rid China of Christianity, which the Boxers blamed for all the ills that had recently befallen the country, including a drought that was causing widespread misery. Another frequent source of misunderstanding is the notion that most of the people the Boxers killed were foreigners, when the vast majority of victims were Chinese Christians.

In addition, the participants did not rely on boxing. The term "Boxer" was coined by the English-language press because the groups involved made use of martial arts fighting techniques, claiming that by employing the right mix of drills and rituals they could make themselves impervious to bullets and defeat the better-armed Western forces. At the height of the crisis, however, the Boxer forces sometimes used weapons, and woodblocks from the time show pitched battles between two armies.

How does the reputation of the crisis differ in China?

In the West and in Japan, the Boxer Rebellion is presented as a tale of the rise and fall of a violent Chinese group. Emphasis is placed on the Boxers' superstitious beliefs, including their notion that they could make themselves impervious to bullets and that railway tracks should be torn up to appease local gods.

In China, by contrast, while the violence and superstitions of the Boxers are sometimes criticized, there is more emphasis on other aspects of the crisis, such as the grievances that led to the insurrection. These injustices included decades of foreign powers' extending their reach into Chinese territory, and the atrocities committed during the "Invasion of the Eight Allied Armies," including the looting of Chinese national treasures and the revenge killing of thousands of northern Chinese. In Chinese accounts now, the Boxer Protocol is described as one of many humiliating and unjustly one-sided treaties that foreign powers forced the Chinese to sign.

Why does this difference in views of the Boxers matter?

The specter of the Boxer Crisis has cast a long shadow over Chinese interactions with foreign countries. Allusions to the events of 1900 have been common whenever conflicts between China and other nations have occurred, but because of how differently the Boxers are viewed, these veer off in opposite directions.

A case in point occurred in May 1999, when NATO bombs hit the Chinese embassy in Belgrade, killing three citizens of the PRC. When Chinese protesters held rowdy demonstrations, hurling objects at the British and US embassies in Beijing and claiming that NATO had intentionally targeted the Chinese embassy in Belgrade, this was decried in some Western media as xenophobic Boxerism. China was once again behaving irrationally, these reports claimed, since the destruction of the Chinese embassy had been a mistake.

Some Chinese, however, invoked memories of 1900 in a completely different manner. The events in Belgrade, they insisted, showed that, once again, Westerners were determined to push China around. The fact that NATO includes some of the same powers (e.g., Britain, the United States, France, etc.) that were part of the coalition of "Eight Allied Armies" who occupied China in 1900 and 1901 gave added force to this very different allusion to the era of the Boxers.

How did Qing rule finally end?

The Qing Dynasty engaged in a last-ditch effort at radical reform after the Boxer crisis that struck many as an effort to do too little too late. It was then toppled in 1911 by a series of loosely connected uprisings and mutinies by imperial troops. These led to the abdication of the last emperor and the establishment of a new Republic of China (ROC), which persists, albeit in a greatly reduced territorial form, on Taiwan. The first president of this country was Sun Yat-sen (1866–1925), who was inaugurated on January 1, 1912.

His installation as China's first president was modeled on that of a Western political leader, and efforts were made to convince foreign powers that everything associated with the dynastic system would be abolished. But Sun also participated in rituals that hearkened back to dynastic transitions and played to the anti-Manchu Han nationalism that had been a part of challenges to the Qing since at least the time of the White Lotus Rebellion. He visited the graves of the Ming emperors, for example, in a move that cast the revolution less as a move forward into uncharted terrain than as an act of revenge for the conquest of the country by foreign invaders from the north.[8]

Is the Chinese Communist Party a new dynasty?

Harrison Salisbury titled his best-selling study of the PRC's first decades *The New Emperors: China in the Era of Mao and Deng*, suggesting that the 1949 revolution that had established the People's Republic, like the 1911 one that had created the ROC, could be seen as yet another playing out of the dynastic cycle.[9] And other Western writers have used imperial metaphors to underline the way that Mao, like emperors of the past, was a political figure who was also viewed as godlike, and to emphasize the secrecy with which the Communist Party leadership shrouds its operations and indeed its daily life—sequestered in a heavily guarded compound known as Zhongnanhai, which is located beside the Forbidden City.

In addition, within China, there are critics of the current regime who employ comparable imagery to discredit figures who claim to represent a revolution that broke completely with the past. For example, during the Tiananmen Uprising of 1989 (about which more later), protesters often described Deng as acting like an "emperor," and one wall poster portrayed him as a modern-day counterpart of the Empress

Dowager Cixi (Tzu Hsi) (1839–1908), who was the mother of one late Qing emperor and the aunt of another and functioned as de facto ruler of China for much of her lifetime. (This imagery derived some of its power from the fact that Deng, though China's paramount leader in 1989, did not hold a high formal title such as party general secretary, president, or prime minister.) In addition, the derisive term "princelings" is often used to refer to the sons of high-ranking party leaders, whom many Chinese view as enjoying unfair advantages and living privileged lives.[10] Perhaps the most famous—or infamous—princeling is Bo Xilai, a charismatic politician who attracted significant popular support as the party secretary of Chongqing municipality before being purged early in 2012 amid a murder scandal and allegations of massive corruption.

This kind of imperial imagery has its value, for it underscores the fact that China is currently beset by some familiar political problems, including high-level corruption rooted in personal access to and sometimes a direct familial relationship with those in high positions. It should not, however, be pushed too far or taken too seriously. In contrast to the ROC, where Chiang Kai-shek was succeeded by his son as president of Taiwan, or for that matter the United States, where two members of the Bush family recently held the same top post in fairly rapid succession, no two top PRC leaders have been related to one another by blood. And there has always, at least since Mao's time, been an oligarchic aspect to the way the Communist Party rules, with a group of top leaders, none of whom is kin to another, sharing power in a manner that differs greatly from that of any dynasty.

More than this, imperial imagery obscures the many ways that the China of today differs from the China of the past. The PRC is changing so quickly that frameworks that suggest it is only able to replicate historical patterns generally do more harm than good.

And yet, the dynastic cycle and the Mandate of Heaven remain concepts worth keeping in mind. As we will see in later sections, some of the things that the leaders of the Communist Party worry about—from the rumblings of popular religious sects to how natural catastrophes are understood—resemble those that caused emperors to worry about how long their own mandate would last.

3

REVOLUTIONS AND REVOLUTIONARIES

Who was Sun Yat-sen?

Sun Yat-sen has been hailed as the founding father of the Republic of China (ROC) and has been likened to George Washington in more than a few Chinese textbooks over the years. Sun has the rare distinction of having been treated as a hero on both sides of the Taiwan straits. In the PRC, streets are named after him and on special occasions his portrait is placed in a prominent spot near Tiananmen Square. In the ROC, at least before the Nationalists were first forced to share power with other parties around the turn of the millennium, his image was a central feature of all major political rituals. This special status is made possible by Sun's association with the overthrow of the Qing, and by the fact that he not only founded the Nationalist Party but also brokered the first United Front (1924–1927), an alliance between the Nationalists and the Communists.

His status in revolutionary history is unique, for those the Communists hail as heroes are usually considered villains on Taiwan and vice versa. Unique, too, was the eclectic ideology he espoused, which combined intense nationalism with a cosmopolitan openness to what foreign creeds had to offer.[1]

In his youth, Sun studied medicine in Hong Kong, traveled widely, and developed reform proposals that he tried, unsuccessfully, to bring to the attention of progressive-minded

Qing officials. His transition from reformer to revolutionary occurred in the 1890s, when he began to work with secret societies and to plan anti-Qing uprisings. In 1905, while in Japan, he founded the Revolutionary Alliance, an organization that would eventually evolve into the Nationalist Party.

Even though Sun was subsequently credited with "leading" the 1911 Revolution, the mutinies and insurrections of October of that year occurred while he was in the United States raising funds for his political ventures. Still, groups with which he was affiliated participated in the upheavals, and he soon returned to China to play a key role in the transition to republican rule.

What happened to Sun after he became president?

Sun's presidency was short-lived. Within a year, Yuan Shikai (Yüan Shih-k'ai) (1859–1916) had nudged him out of office. Yuan was a former Qing official and general who had shifted his allegiance to the Revolution in 1911, and then in 1912 insisted that he would continue to support the new order only if he was made its president. Lacking an army of his own, Sun felt he had to step aside, though he immediately set about trying to develop a power base from which to reclaim leadership of the country.

Sun never managed to regain control of China, which was run by a succession of military strongmen (sometimes called "warlords") until his death in 1925. But the Nationalist Party he founded would, under his successor, Chiang Kai-shek, end up governing China for more than two decades and Taiwan for another half century.

What was the "Warlord era"?

Yuan's assumption of power ushered in a decade-and-a-half-long period during which one or another military strongman was officially designated as China's president. Yet in reality they shared control of the country with a number of strong regional leaders.

Each of these men had an army and, by virtue of this, effectively controlled a part of the country. Some of the warlords, including Yuan, dreamed of becoming emperors and establishing new dynasties. And even though none of these efforts to formally restore the imperial system proved successful, the period was, in political terms, a bit of a throwback to the final years of Qing rule, save for the overlay of some of the trappings of a republic in, for example, the titles held by officials.[2]

What was the May 4th movement?

The warlords' abandonment of the revolutionary legacy of 1911 did not go unchallenged. Sun Yat-sen set up operations in Guangzhou, at the head of a revamped Revolutionary Alliance, now rechristened as the Nationalist Party. As he dreamed of regaining control of the country, intellectuals agitated for an end to warlord rule and looked to the outside world (Japan, Russia, and the West) for ideas and strategies that could be brought to China to help get the revolutionary project back on track.

Radical teachers and students in Beijing and Shanghai were particularly active in both intellectual exploration, which took such forms as translating theoretical and literary works into Chinese and experimenting with new forms of writing, and political mobilization. Their most important collective actions involved protesting the willingness of the warlords to capitulate to demands that foreign powers (especially Japan) made to extend their territorial and economic reach within China. Most importantly, these students and young professors spearheaded an anti-warlord and anti-imperialist drive known as the May 4th movement.

This political struggle, which was linked to the anti-Confucian New Culture movement discussed earlier, was one of the events that truly changed China. Named for the date in 1919 when a rowdy protest was held in what would later become Tiananmen Square, the specific trigger for it was the way that China was treated during the Paris Peace Conference after World War I.

The Allies had claimed that one outcome of the war would be that all nations would have the right to determine their own fates, and that with the defeat of Germany the age of empires would come to an end. Since China had, albeit belatedly, joined the Allies, there seemed good reason to hope that parts of China formerly under German control would return to Beijing's rule. Instead, however, the Conference planned to cede these territories, on the Shandong Peninsula, to Japan in the Treaty of Versailles—and, much to the anger of Chinese students, the warlord government seemed unwilling to fight or even challenge this decision.

On May 4, 1919, students rampaged through Beijing calling for Shandong's return to Chinese control and the dismissal from office of three officials viewed as corrupt and pro-Japanese. After destroying the house of one of these officials, some of these students were arrested and beaten up; one later died from his wounds. Due in part to the traditional high regard in which scholars were held, members of all urban social classes joined the protests.

The May 4th movement reached its peak in Shanghai in early June with a general strike that paralyzed China's main financial and commercial center. When it achieved most of its goals, it was hailed as a victorious struggle.

In the end, the Treaty of Versailles took effect unaltered. But the students arrested in the original protest were all released, the three hated officials were dismissed from office, and the Chinese delegation to the Paris Peace Conference refused to sign the Paris accord.[3]

Who was the most important radical writer of the May 4th era?

Many authors contributed to the intellectual ferment of the time, but the one whose literary legacy is richest and most important is Lu Xun. He is also, arguably, the most important author of the early 1900s whose works remain little known in the West, despite the regular appearance of new translations of his stories.[4] His importance is due partly to the range and power of his writings. He was a highly accomplished essayist and author of major short stories, such as the searing anti-Confucian parable "Diary of a Madman" (which portrays traditional Chinese values as soul-destroying) and a novella, "The Real Story of Ah Q" (which satirizes the 1911 Revolution as a struggle that claimed it could change everything, yet often seemed to do little besides alter the names of the posts held by local officials who bullied the people).

Another way in which Lu Xun is unusually significant is that his publications permanently altered the Chinese political vocabulary, infusing it with new terms such as "Ah Qism," derived from the tendency of the eponymous anti-hero of Lu Xun's novella to change failures into victories when retelling the tale of his exploits, which continue to be used.

To be ignorant of Lu Xun, therefore, can make it hard to follow some Chinese political debates. Though Lu Xun has been compared to many other Western writers over the years, from Gogol (an author who inspired him) to Nietzsche (one study of Lu Xun dubs him China's "Gentle Nietzsche"), he is China's closest counterpart to Orwell. Just as those unfamiliar with Orwell will be confused by English editorials that include casual references to "Big Brother," "Newspeak," and other terms from *1984*, without knowing who Ah Q was or what the implications of describing traditional values as cannibalistic are, some of the subtleties in Chinese political debates will go over one's head.

A final reason for Lu Xun's importance is that, though for most of his life he was fiercely independent of dogmatisms of the Right and the Left, he tended to side with the Communist Party in the years immediately before his death, though he never actually joined the organization. This allowed Mao to elevate him to the status of a revolutionary saint within the

People's Republic. But, as Mao himself once admitted, had Lu Xun lived past 1949 he would likely have ended up running afoul of the new regime. By dying early, however, the way was cleared for the Communist Party to use him, and his stories became, at certain points between the 1950s and 1970s, virtually the only Chinese works of fiction from the first half of the 20th century that could be published and read freely.[5]

Here, again, an (albeit twisted) parallel with Orwell is noteworthy. Orwell, in life, was caustic about the hypocritical aspects of all isms, yet after death he was often made a one-dimensional poster boy for the anti-Communist Cold War Right.

How does the Communist Party view the May 4th era?

Lu Xun is by no means the only figure from the May 4th period celebrated in the PRC, for many future leaders of the Communist Revolution, including Mao, were linked to the struggle of 1919. In fact, once in power, the Communist Party turned the anniversary of the 1919 protests into a national holiday honoring youthful patriotism because it is seen as an event that paved the way for the founding of the Chinese Communist Party (CCP).

It is certainly true that the popular ferment of 1919, which inspired many youths to think that collective action could help get the revolution back on course, was crucial to the establishment of the CCP. So, too, was the outbreak of the Russian Revolution in 1917, which was hailed as being of epochal importance in the major New Culture movement journal, *New Youth*, and fueled a dramatic rise within China in interest in Marxism, after a period when radicals had been more drawn to anarchist ideas.

There is debate now over whether the CCP was born in 1920—when important meetings of some future leaders of the organization occurred—or 1921, the date the PRC officially treats as the year of the party's birth. In either version of the story, the central players in its early life included radical Beijing professors, such as "New Youth" founders Li Dazhao (Li Ta-chao) (1888–1927), the author of an influential essay hailing the "Victory of Bolshevism" in Russia as a great thing, and Chen Duxiu (Ch'en Tu-hsiu) (1879–1942), a mentor to Mao, who advised the students involved in the 1919 demonstrations. Other early members of the Communist Party besides Mao who were involved in May 4th protests included Zhou Enlai (Chou En-lai) (1898–1976) and his wife Deng Yingchao (Teng Ying-ch'ao) (1904–1992), who was always much less famous than her husband internationally but was for decades an influential figure in the PRC.

Why was the example of the Russian Revolution so important?

The Russian Revolution's inspirational role for Chinese activists was crucial, not just because of the appeal of its ideals of social equality but also because of the fact that it occurred in a country that was a late-comer to industrialization and was seen as backward. Members of the May 4th generation were not only critical of Confucian hierarchies but also eager for their country to regain its former stature as a great power. Russia alone seemed to have found a recipe to help remake a country domestically and increase its international prestige.[6]

What was the First United Front?

The Communist Party did not have much of an impact on Chinese politics until Sun Yat-sen, who was attracted by Moscow's criticism of Western imperialism and the emphasis Lenin had put on the role that a tightly disciplined vanguard party could play in moving a country forward, invited the CCP to join the Nationalists in a "united front" that would try to both unseat the warlords and fight foreign encroachments. Members of the fledgling CCP accepted the invitation readily;

some, including a young Mao, would even hold positions in both parties for a time.

The first major mass movement accompanying this United Front, which lasted from 1924 until 1927 and later became known as the "First United Front" to differentiate it from a second collaboration between the Nationalists and Communists, broke out in 1925. It was called the May 30th movement, was seen by some as picking up where the May 4th movement left off, and was triggered by the police in Shanghai's main foreign-run enclave firing into a crowd of Chinese protesters who were demonstrating against the mistreatment of Chinese workers in Japanese mills located within Shanghai.

Why was the May 30th movement important?

This anti-imperialist struggle, like its predecessor of 1919, spread from being a single-city protest to being a national one and culminated in a general strike that paralyzed Shanghai. It did not achieve as many of its stated goals as the May 4th movement; the unmet demands of May 30th protesters included that Chinese workers at foreign factories be given the right to form unions and that all foreign-run sections of treaty ports be returned to Chinese control. Nevertheless, the propaganda and mobilization work done by activists brought many new converts into both the Nationalist and Communist organizations, making the latter, for the first time, a force to be reckoned with in Chinese politics.[7] This development paved the way for the end of warlord rule after the Northern Expedition.

What was the Northern Expedition?

The Northern Expedition was launched in 1926 from Sun's southern power base in Guangdong (Kwangtung) Province. A joint army of Nationalists and Communists, led by Chiang Kai-shek, marched northward toward Beijing and, beginning in 1926, waged a series of battles against the armies of regional militarists in which the Nationalists were victorious.

In 1927 the Chinese-run sections of Shanghai (as with other treaty ports, only some parts of the city were under foreign control) easily fell to the Northern Expedition's troops, thanks to a series of worker uprisings led by the CCP, which prepared the groundwork for the arrival of Chiang Kai-shek's soldiers.

Later that same year, Chiang, who had succeeded Sun as head of the Nationalists after Sun's death in March 1925, took the nearby city of Nanjing and proclaimed it the real capital of the republic (its name means "southern capital," and it had been a seat of government before). Then, in 1928, Chiang's forces took Beijing (whose name means "northern capital") and renamed it Beiping ("northern peace") to show that the political center remained in the south.[8]

Who was Chiang Kai-shek?

Chiang was often called simply "Generalissimo," because of his role as leader of the Northern Expedition forces and his military background and bearing. An enigmatic figure, before committing himself to the revolution he had joined a secret society, established ties with the Green Gang (a powerful organized-crime syndicate based in Shanghai), and received military training in Japan.

He developed close personal ties to Sun Yat-sen via common revolutionary activities. These took on an added dimension when Chiang married Song Meiling (Soong May-ling) (1898–2003). An American-educated Christian, Song Meiling was the sister of Sun's widow, Song Qingling (Soong Ch'ing-ling) (1893–1981), who never formally joined the Communist Party but remained on the Mainland after 1949 and served as an official.

Aside from his skills as a military strategist, the generalissimo proved very effective at forming alliances that helped him navigate the factional politics of the Nationalist Party.

These were complex because several people thought that they should succeed Sun as leader of the organization.

Whether he ever shared Sun's conviction that the cause of the Chinese Revolution was best served by an alliance with Communists is unclear, but by late 1926 Chiang felt that the United Front was a mistake. In April 1927, with help from the Green Gang, he carried out a vicious purge of Communist Party members in Shanghai, imprisoning and killing some of the very people who had helped deliver the Chinese-run parts of the city to the Northern Expedition forces.

From that point on, until his death in 1975, he treated the Communists as a great threat to China's future. For purely practical purposes, Chiang was forced to ally with the Communists again during the Second United Front (1937–1945). (He was pressured into the arrangement, after being taken hostage in Xi'an in 1936, held by a warlord who thought China's only hope for salvation lay in unity between warring factions.) But Chiang's anti-Communism was deeply felt and enduring, and he continued to argue that, as he put it, the Japanese were only a "disease of the skin," while the Communists were a "disease of the heart"—that is, ultimately the graver threat to Chinese national survival.

What was the Long March?

Chiang Kai-shek's "White Terror" purges almost succeeded in eliminating the Communist Party in 1927. The Communists, however, proved impossible to eradicate completely.

Some members of the organization avoided detection and operated underground cells within cities held by the Nationalists, while others escaped to rural Communist base areas. In the early 1930s, Jiang tried several times to encircle those base areas and destroy the main clusters of remaining Communists; to escape this fate the CCP abandoned its temporary headquarters in the southern province of Jiangxi and began a torturous trek northward that became known as the Long March.

This 1934–1935 trek ended with the Communists setting up new base areas in Shaanxi Province, the most famous in Yan'an, where they began to experiment with policies, such as bold land redistribution campaigns, that eventually won them support from many poor Chinese and also greatly impressed some Western visitors (most famously the American journalist Edgar Snow).[9] In official PRC histories, the Long March is treated as an event of mythic significance and proportions, and it is easy to see why. The odds against a straggling band of guerrillas escaping from the much better-armed Nationalist forces while traveling over often-treacherous terrain to safety some six thousand miles from their starting point are staggering. The journey involved eighty-six thousand people, who traversed six thousand miles in just over a year, crossing eighteen mountain ranges and twenty-four rivers. In the end, only some eight thousand of those who began the trip survived.[10]

Had the Long March failed, the CCP would have ceased to play a role in Chinese politics and history, but the march had another significant outcome: it was during this epic exodus that Mao consolidated his position as supreme leader of the party, thanks in part to his vision of guerrilla warfare as the way to fight the Nationalists being endorsed as the best military strategy to pursue. Though he would turn against some of his comrades in arms from the Long March in "rectification campaigns" (in effect, purges) of the early to mid-1940s and break with others after the founding of the PRC, Mao's closest allies from the 1930s on tended to be fellow Long March veterans. If a Communist leader had spent the 1930s and 1940s doing underground work in a "White" city controlled by the Nationalists rather than in a "Red" area like Yan'an—and hence been further from Mao's direct influence and closer to the temptations of a mode of life he viewed as "bourgeois" and decadent—they were vulnerable after 1949 to charges of political impurity. In particular, they were more likely to be dubbed "capitalist roaders," beaten up by Red Guards fiercely loyal to Mao, subjected to public criticism, and even tortured during the Cultural Revolution—about which more below.[11]

What was the Rape of Nanjing?

The period of the Japanese occupation, which began with Japan taking over parts of Manchuria in 1931, remains a bitterly remembered one in China. A particularly significant event in this regard was the Rape of Nanjing, which unfolded in late 1937 and early 1938. According to one recent US survey of Chinese history, during a short horrific period in Nanjing, "an estimated 200,000 to 300,000 Chinese were killed" and "an estimated 20,000 women were raped" by Japanese soldiers.[12]

The Japanese invasion in general (there were atrocities committed in many parts of the country) and the Rape of Nanjing in particular continue to bedevil Sino–Japanese relations. This is in part because some textbooks approved for use in Japan downplay the extent of the atrocities, and Tokyo, though officially expressing regret for the invasions of the 1930s and 1940s, has stopped short of carrying out a thoroughgoing repudiation of all aspects of its World War II behavior such as Germany undertook.

How did the Communists beat the Nationalists?

Many factors contributed to Mao's defeat of Chiang. For example, the way that World War II played out fostered an image of the Communists as devoted patriots. The Nationalists and the Communists had allied to fight Japan from 1937 on, but many Chinese were left feeling that the latter organization was more wholeheartedly committed to fighting imperialism than was the former, which had trouble shaking its reputation for being corrupt and led by a man obsessed with the idea that Communism was as big a threat as foreign invaders.

When the Japanese finally surrendered, many hoped a period of peace and stability would begin. This was not to be.

The rapprochement between the Nationalists and Communists, which had long been strained, collapsed completely within months of Japan's mid-1945 surrender. A civil war broke out almost immediately, lasting until 1949, when Mao's Red Army, known as the People's Liberation Army (PLA), took control of several key cities. These included Shanghai and Beiping, whose name the Communists changed back to Beijing, signaling that it was once again China's capital.

Throughout the Civil War, pitched battles were fought in the countryside, and more symbolic struggles, via propaganda and demonstrations, were waged in the cities. The Communists promised that if they won they would redistribute land, and this gained them support in many villages, especially since word had circulated that bold land reform programs (in which landlords were stripped of their holdings and sometimes beaten and even killed) had been occurring for years in areas under the Communist Party's control. Meanwhile, disgust with official corruption, Nationalist infighting, government censorship drives, crackdowns on urban demonstrations, and a sense that the generalissimo was too beholden to the United States alienated many intellectuals in the cities.

The United States backed the Nationalists (with some reservations), while the Soviet Union backed the Communists (likewise with ambivalence), as was expected as the Cold War got under way. Chiang later insisted that the key to Mao's victory was Moscow's backing, but equally or more important was Chiang's failure to run the country effectively in the late 1940s, most evident in runaway inflation of such staggering proportions that city dwellers sometimes needed wheelbarrows full of nearly worthless currency to buy rice.[13]

Given how disliked by intellectuals the Nationalists had become by the late 1940s, the reputation that the Communists had earned among workers and farmers as an organization that championed the interests of the common people, and the desire of Chinese of all classes for a time of peace, it is no wonder that the end of the Civil War was seen by many as a very welcome development. The year 1949 was hailed in the Communist Party press at the time as a moment of "liberation," a term that continues to be used to this day in the PRC as a shorthand for that year. This is surely what it felt like to many people at that point, though landlords were bound to see it as a fearful rather than welcome thing that the Communist Party had taken control of the country. And though other groups would also soon have misgivings about the turn the nation had taken, in the early 1950s, with the country at peace and living standards rising, many continued to feel that China was moving in a positive direction.

What role have mass campaigns played in the People's Republic of China?

Throughout the first decades of Communist Party rule in China, mass campaigns were an important feature of daily life. These drives, which were used to publicize and ensure compliance with new policies, would remain important as well during the two years immediately following Mao's death, when Hua Guofeng (1921–2008) held power. After Hua was demoted and Deng took charge in 1978, campaigns became less common, but they have sometimes played a significant role, even in the Reform era (1978–).

The content of these campaigns has varied greatly. Their formats, however, have been similar. High officials give speeches and leading newspapers publish editorials spelling out the goals of the drive; city streets are covered with banners containing key slogans, as are public buildings in urban and rural settings; party representatives, the heads of neighborhood associations (important grassroots-level authority figures during the early decades of the PRC in particular), and leaders of the individual *danwei* (work units) that structure so much of social life in China (many people live in housing, for example, that these *danwei* provide) take charge of getting their subordinates to participate in rallies and other activities.

And sometimes individuals or activities representing ideas or practices the campaign is meant to counteract are singled out for criticism. According to a top party official, early campaigns were an effort, above all, to ensure that the goals of the party were internalized, to get the people to "emancipate themselves step by step, instead of [the government] imposing revolution on the masses or bestowing victory on the masses as a favor."[14] Among important early mass campaigns was the Land Reform drive, which extended to new areas the redistribution of landlords' holdings and included verbal and physical assaults on anyone viewed as belonging to the vilified landlord class. This campaign had begun in Yan'an and other areas under Communist Party control before 1949. But the first PRC nationwide movement was the one designed to publicize and gain compliance with the New Marriage Law of 1950 (about which more below).

What was the Resist America, Support Korea campaign?

The goal of the Resist America, Support Korea campaign was to solidify the reputation of the party as a patriotic organization determined to ensure that China would never again be pushed around by foreign powers. It began as soon as the Korean War (1950–1953) started.

This first "hot war" of the Cold War era, which pitted allies of the Soviet Union against allies of the United States, ended in a stalemate, creating the division between Communist North Korea and non-Communist South Korea that continues to this day. Mao claimed, however, that the war represented a great victory for China. The PRC contributed the largest number of troops to the North Korean cause, and more Chinese died during the struggle than members of any other foreign population, with Mao's own son among the casualties. Propaganda posters, films, and stories celebrated the heroics of Chinese soldiers, while those on the home front attended rallies against American imperialism and donated money to support the war effort. At the same time, the CCP government embarked upon an intense effort to root out alleged spies, targeting those with connections to foreign governments, businesses, churches, and schools, as well as Chiang's Nationalists.

The "victory," according to Mao, lay in the Communist forces' ability to prevent the Americans and their allies from taking control of the entire Korean peninsula. This proved that China could hold its own against apparently superior powers. But another sort of "victory" was that enjoyed by the CCP, which had used the campaign to consolidate its control over both businesses and people throughout the country.[15]

What was the Hundred Flowers campaign?

The Hungarian Uprising of 1956, which was suppressed only with Moscow's help, sent shock waves throughout the Communist world. This revolt exposed as a myth the idea that the Communist leaderships of all countries linked to the Soviet Union—a category that included China at that point, since aid and advisers from Moscow were playing important roles in the nation—enjoyed broad popular support. It also exposed as illusory the notion that the state socialist lands of Central and Eastern Europe were allies as opposed to merely satellites of the Soviet Union.

The Chinese response to this included Mao's call for a loosening of the taboo on pointing out mistakes made by the party and any problems with its official ideology, the idea being that the regime could be strengthened through constructive criticism. The slogan used for this 1957 initiative was "Let a Hundred Flowers Bloom and a Hundred Schools of Thought Contend," an allusion to the distant Warring States period, when proponents of Confucian, Daoist, Legalist, and many other visions of morality and statecraft had competed for the attention and patronage of local rulers. Soon professors and students around the country were writing memorials and putting up wall posters calling for change.

The Hundred Flowers campaign has been interpreted as a cynical effort by Mao to smoke out all intellectuals with dangerous ideas. A competing interpretation holds that it was meant to demonstrate that the party was popular enough and firmly enough in control that it could benefit from advice, and by doing this further increase its support among intellectuals, who would feel better about aiding a regime that allowed more freedom of speech. In this view, the crackdown on critics that soon came was a response to the unexpectedly harsh nature of the commentary unleashed.

In either case, the end result was that a brief flourishing of open discussion was followed by a series of purges. These purges were known as the Anti-Rightist campaign.

What happened during the Anti-Rightist campaign?

The Anti-Rightist campaign was a drive used to inculcate intellectual orthodoxy. Anyone who expressed or was simply accused of harboring unorthodox views risked being designated a "counterrevolutionary" and "enemy of the people," subjected to public criticism, and sent to a prison camp. Once incarcerated, these "Rightists" would experience a period of either "reform through labor" or "reeducation" that, if successful, would allow them to reenter society. They would never be able to fully shake the stigma of having once been labeled a Rightist, since a file was kept on every citizen of the PRC, which included notes on the individual's political history—a dossier system that has still not been completely abandoned.

In addition to those who actually expressed criticism of the new regime, some people suffered during the Anti-Rightist campaign for quite different reasons. Some were labeled Rightists because individuals who held grudges against them or wanted to burnish their own reputations for political rectitude concocted tales of the targeted person's failings. Others

were singled out because the central authorities told local officials to fulfill specific quotas of Rightists because Mao had
made statements that a certain percentage of the population
was composed of enemies of the revolution trying to hide
their beliefs.

How did women fare during the first decade of the PRC?

It is telling that one of the first pieces of the new regime's leg-
islation was the New Marriage Law of 1950, given the central
role of family relations in Confucian thought and the bias
against women within late imperial society. This bias had been
expressed through everything from demands for widows to
remain chaste, to girls being pressured to bind their feet (in a
painful process that among other things limited their physical
mobility), to only men being able to take official examinations.
It is true that some noteworthy moves were made during the
Republican period (1912–1949) to remake gender and family
relations. Most notably, women were granted the right to vote
in 1947—admittedly something of a Pyrrhic victory, given
that in the Civil War era elections had so little value—and
foot binding (never a universal practice and something that
varied widely between regions and across class and ethnic
lines) became much less common and increasingly frowned
upon by the state. But once Chiang Kai-shek took power, the
celebration of Confucianism, interpreted in very traditional
ways, put a check on moves toward greater equality between
the sexes.

Introducing a new marriage system, in which family elders
were not the key determinants of who would marry whom
and men and women would be treated equally, was seen by
the Communists as a powerful way to change social and political relations within villages, and it signaled that a truly new
order had begun—that this revolution would lead to much
more than simply changing what local bullies were called.[16]

The Marriage Law campaign championed the idea that betrothals should be between freely consenting individuals, rather than arranged by family elders, and that, once married, husbands and wives would be treated the same under the law (even having equal ability to seek divorce, something that under the old system had been much easier for a man than for a woman to do). Though the New Marriage Law did not officially require this, one symbolically significant shift that accompanied its implementation was the substitution of the party for the husband's family in ritual aspects of weddings, represented by the fact that in post-1949 marriages, a portrait of Mao was often placed where images of lineage ancestors had been in pre-1949 weddings, with new couples bowing before it as they had once bowed before the husband's parents.

Mao and the CCP proclaimed that "women hold up half the sky," promising the dawn of a new era in gender relations. In some respects, life for Chinese women did improve during the early PRC years. Many assumed positions of responsibility in their local party units, while others found themselves lauded as "model workers" for their labor productivity. A campaign promoting safe childbirth also yielded dramatic improvements in maternal and infant mortality. Yet, while many women joined the labor force and began working in offices, in factories, or, toward the end of the 1950s, on collective farms, they remained the primary caregivers for their families, often working a "second shift" to complete their household's cooking, cleaning, washing, sewing, and childrearing. As a result, Chinese women might remember the first decade of the PRC as a time of progress, but also as one of exhaustion.[17]

What sort of people were Mao and his main allies?

Mao was born into a middling sort of rural family (his father had enough money to employ a laborer and to educate his sons), and in his youth he gravitated toward radical politics.

He did this first within his native Hunan Province and later in Beijing, where he worked as a librarian and was influenced greatly by progressive teachers, especially Chen Duxiu, who had begun to promote anarchist and Marxist ideas. His most significant early writings included a report on the Hunan peasant movement, in which he stressed the party's need to learn from the actions of rural activists (rather than assume, in a more orthodox Marxist fashion, that farmers were an inherently backward group who needed guidance from urbanites); claimed that extreme tactics and great violence were often a necessary part of revolutionary settings (this is where his famous statement that "revolution is not a dinner party" appears); and noted that women were uniquely oppressed in China (not only suffering from class injustices but also having power wielded over them by male relatives).

Mao rose to power within the party during the Long March, as already noted, and when the PRC was founded, his supremacy was symbolized by the fact that it was he who stood atop Tiananmen (the Gate of Heavenly Peace) and proclaimed the establishment of the new country. The giant portrait of his face, which still hangs near that spot, is a reminder of his role as the first paramount leader of the PRC. Mao insisted that he did not want to be the subject of a "personality cult," and even prohibited celebrations of his birthday, and yet he was elevated to a godlike status within the PRC during his lifetime. Since the official version of Communist Party history promoted from 1949 until 1976 cast him as the central player in each and every defining moment of the revolution from the early 1920s on, unfairly downplaying the contributions of many others, celebrations of holidays such as those marking the anniversaries of the founding of the party (July 1), the founding of the Red Army (August 1), and even the founding of the country (October 1) became, in effect, as much celebrations of Mao as an individual as of the collectivities they ostensibly honored.

Mao's closest associates, as mentioned earlier, were mostly other Long March veterans. These included Zhou Enlai, who was known for his diplomatic skills, and Zhu De (Chu Te) (1886–1976), the second-most-important PLA leader. These were all people who had worked most closely with Mao in Yan'an, where the policies that would guide the early years of the PRC were first developed and tested, a village that became a pilgrimage site for those who viewed these leaders as sacred figures.

Like Mao, many of his allies had first become politically active during or just before the New Culture movement and had been involved in anti-imperialist and anti-warlord protests of the 1910s. Some had studied abroad in their youths (Zhou spent time in France, as had Deng Xiaoping, also a Long March veteran), while others, including Mao, did not leave the country for the first time until much later in life (in his case not until going to Moscow after 1949)—if they ever left it at all. In addition to the Long March veterans, there were some high officials, such as Liu Shaoqi (Liu Shao-ch'i) (1898–1969), Mao's heir apparent in the 1950s and early 1960s, who spent the 1930s and 1940s in urban centers controlled by the Nationalists, where they sought to organize workers and carry out underground propaganda efforts on behalf of the Communist cause.

How were Mao's writings viewed?

Mao's speeches and essays were initially treated simply as the products of the most influential Chinese interpreter of Marxism. Soon, however, they began to take on the function of Holy Scripture, becoming texts that were studied compulsively, memorized, and used as the final arbiters of morality and immorality.

This contributed to and was an expression of Mao's general elevation to godlike status, which was visually represented in the many statues, giant portraits, and innumerable posters that celebrated his accomplishments and treated him as the embodiment of the revolution and indeed of the New

China—a term constantly used to refer to the nation established in 1949.

His writings covered a wide spectrum of issues, as he crafted theoretical texts that endorsed his modification of Marxism relating to the revolutionary potential of peasants, wrote poems in classical style, and stressed the importance of guerrilla warfare as a method for numerically and militarily weaker groups to attain power. Always a critic of Western imperialism, from the late 1950s on he also devoted much of his writing to denouncing the Soviet Union (a split between Moscow and Beijing, tied to disputed borders and to different views of the international Communist movement, had opened up by then) for shifting from revolutionary to revisionist positions. China's version of Communism, not the Soviet Union's, he insisted, provided the best model for revolutionaries in developing countries to follow because it emphasized the revolutionary potential of the peasantry and stressed anti-imperialist action.

What was the Great Leap Forward?

By the late 1950s, Mao had become impatient. He wanted China to move more rapidly toward achieving the egalitarian utopia of true Communism—and to show the world that his country was more than just one of many junior partners in the global Communist movement led by the Soviet Union.

This prompted him to push for a bold new project, which was designed to convince his followers at home and foreign observers that China was capable of excelling in certain areas and not just following along behind the Soviets; moreover, he wanted to demonstrate that it could even become equal to or surpass the strongest countries of the West. He called for abandoning go-slow policies, based on step-by-step moves toward higher levels of collectivization, and pursuing instead a "Great Leap Forward," which would be achieved through rapid collectivization and bold campaigns to increase crop yields and raise steel production, all intended to help China achieve full-blown Communism before the Soviet Union and gain economic parity with the West.

The initial results of the program seemed impressive, as enormously high crop yields were reported. And reports filled the newspapers of the "happier collective life" that peasants were enjoying as they made the most of the new group "dining rooms, kindergartens, nurseries, sewing groups, barber shops, public baths, happy homes for the aged," and so forth provided by communes.[18] Beneath the surface, however, the fault lines of an impending disaster were forming. Fearing that the central authorities would punish them for being insufficiently supportive of Mao's directives if they failed to report exciting results, local officials grossly overstated the size of crop yields. And in order to boost steel production figures, useful farm implements were melted down to create useless (except for bragging purposes) hunks of metal. In addition, some pseudoscientific innovations endorsed by Mao, such as planting crops closer together to boost harvest levels, were dismal failures.

When these problems were compounded by bad weather, the result was the most lethal famine in world history: lasting until 1961, it claimed at least 20 million lives, perhaps closer to 30 million. It hit the young unusually hard: the median age of those dying in China plunged from a 1957 level of 17.6 years to a 1963 level of 9.7 (i.e., half of the dead that year were younger than 10). As historian Jonathan Spence put it, "the Great Leap Forward, launched in the name of strengthening the nation by summoning all the people's energies, had turned back on itself and ended by devouring its young."[19]

What was the Cultural Revolution?

After the Great Leap disaster, Mao temporarily lost his position as China's paramount leader. Though Mao was still officially venerated as the nation's greatest thinker, the actual running of the country was taken over by Liu Shaoqi, Deng Xiaoping, and other party leaders thought of as more pragmatic, less utopian. The Cultural Revolution, which remains one of the least fully understood events in modern Chinese history, both within and outside of China, was largely an effort by Mao to reclaim a position of centrality by going around the bureaucracy of the party and leading a mass movement.

The struggle began with Mao (who worried that the Revolution was ossifying) issuing militant statements and then presiding over massive rallies by passionate loyalist youths known as "Red Guards," who verbally—and sometimes physically—attacked anyone they viewed as insufficiently devoted to their hero, sometimes literally beating these "enemies of the people" to death. Mostly high school and college students, the Red Guards often targeted teachers and school administrators they accused of being too conservative or not respectful enough of Mao's teachings.

The years that followed were marked by back-to-back political campaigns, in which many high-ranking leaders became targets of angry crowds. It was a time of chaotic purges and counterpurges (when the victims of one wave could become the bullies of the next). Liu Shaoqi went from being Mao's chosen successor to the target of a mass campaign, a fate that eventually also befell his replacement, Lin Biao (1907–1971). During this period, campuses were closed and intellectuals sent to the countryside to purify themselves by working the land.

The Cultural Revolution was a time of street clashes and rural violence, in which many innocent people suffered, whether from having their reputations damaged or being harassed so intensely that they killed themselves. It was a time of utopian hopes that turned into dark nightmares, an era when children turned on their parents and friends betrayed friends, swept up in the ideological fervor of a particular campaign or simply a desire for self-preservation; in this setting the safest thing to do was often to find others to denounce to prove one's own virtue. The campaign had many of the same characteristics as a fundamentalist religious movement, with Mao in the role of prophet and his works becoming the sole text allowed to define moral purity. It was also, in part, an effort by youths who had grown up surrounded by films and posters that told them the only way to live a meaningful life was to take part in epic acts of upheaval to create new equivalents to the Long March and Yan'an period—and this element of reenactment manifested itself in Red Guard travels around China (framed as efforts to spread Mao's teachings and "share revolutionary experiences" with one another), sometimes by train and sometimes on foot (e.g., walking through terrain that Mao had traversed three or four decades earlier).

What was the Gang of Four?

The Gang of Four was a term used for Mao's wife, and later widow, Jiang Qing (1914–1991), and three of her allies. Jiang and Mao had been married since the Yan'an years, but until the mid-1960s, she remained mostly absent from elite politics. This changed, though, when she began promoting radical literature and performing arts at the outset of the Cultural Revolution. Exerting a great deal of power near the end of the Cultural Revolution, she and the other Gang of Four members became targets of mass campaigns and were imprisoned soon after Mao's death in 1976.

The Gang of Four was scapegoated for the mistakes of the Cultural Revolution in a manner that partially mitigated Mao's responsibility for the *luan* (turmoil) of the era. They are presented in official histories as scheming, unprincipled opportunists who took advantage of their connections to Mao to carry out a nefarious plot to destroy the country and assume absolute power. Their method was to label as "Rightists" anyone they disliked or felt was a competitor (e.g., Deng Xiaoping), while embracing an exaggerated form of "leftism" that claimed to be ultra-revolutionary but that in fact endangered the revolution. Jiang, who committed suicide in prison in 1991, is now mostly remembered in China as a villainous woman whose self-interested schemes could have toppled the state, demonized as a "dragon lady" in the style of imperial wives during China's dynastic past.[20]

Why hasn't Mao been repudiated by China's current leaders?

Varying assessments of Mao have always existed, and still do exist, of course, outside of China; there are even places (such as Nepal) where Maoist guerrillas treat his writings as gospel. Still, of late it has become very common outside of China to refer to Mao as a counterpart to Hitler, largely because of the damage his policies did to the country during the Great Leap and the Cultural Revolution.

The Hitler analogy is a misleading one in many ways, but it must be understood before its flaws can be explained. It is an important issue to address because if Mao is thought of simply as a Hitler with Chinese characteristics, then it is bound to seem bizarre and disturbing, to say the least, that his face appears on PRC banknotes, his body lies preserved in Tiananmen Square, and references to carrying forward "Mao Zedong Thought" (along with "Deng Xiaoping Theory," the oddly titled "Three Represents" concept of Jiang Zemin, and the "Harmonious Society" ideas of Hu Jintao) still show up in National Day slogans.

The best place to begin our examination of the popular (in the West and Taiwan) but misleadingly one-dimensional image of China's former leader as an embodiment of evil, pure and simple, is with Jung Chang and Jon Halliday's best-selling biography, *Mao: The Unknown Story.*[21] Published in 2005, it has become the most famous biography of Mao. Prior to its appearance, some Westerners already thought it odd that Mao had not been more thoroughly repudiated in the PRC, especially since the current CCP leaders had gone so far to distance themselves from some of his policies and from his fiercely anti-capitalist and pro-class struggle rhetoric. Since the book's publication and the flurry of media attention that accompanied it, though, this sense of bewilderment has increased dramatically.

This reaction is because, among its distinctions, this book is the English-language biography of Mao that provides the most negative view of him. Not content to locate Mao within a triumvirate of evil that includes Hitler and Stalin (as writers before them had done), Chang and Halliday go further, presenting him as in some ways the vilest of the three. The book includes a controversial claim that is now routinely repeated as a simple statement of fact: Mao was responsible for 70 million peacetime deaths, more than any other leader in history.

This figure is based on a questionable chain of arguments that claims he "killed" everyone who died during the Great Leap famine, instead of simply implementing misguided policies that precipitated a catastrophic event. Furthermore, every victim of the purges and mass campaigns from the 1950s through the mid-1970s who died in prison or committed suicide, in addition to those slain during the civil war–like Cultural Revolution clashes, represents a "peacetime" death to be laid at his door.

The number itself is impossible to verify, partly because it is difficult to separate starvation from other causes of death in famine years. It is also impossible to neatly separate mortality resulting from political violence from death caused by old age or illness during times of civil strife. In addition, a focus solely on catastrophe leaves out of the picture completely the achievements of the first decades of the PRC: the fact remains that, despite all of the horrors of the Great Leap Forward, Mao's time in power saw life expectancy within China jump from roughly thirty-five years to seventy, while illiteracy declined even more sharply (from approximately 80 percent to under 10 percent).

The book, which is packed with detailed descriptions of acts of violence and a great deal of lurid prose, portrays Mao as behaving, from youth onward, as a heartless Machiavellian figure. He never even truly believed in Marxism, the authors claim, but embraced the creed simply as a way to gain power. Moreover, they assert that, late in life, Mao became a bloodthirsty and sexually depraved tyrant who interacted only with sycophants.

Overall, their book presents Mao as more demonic than human. He was someone who, the authors insist, had no capacity for love and never felt a single twinge of remorse for his actions—though how exactly this can be "proven" without the magical ability to peer into a subject's soul, or at least interview him, as they could not, is left unexplained.

What is the alternative to viewing Mao as a monster?

There are many alternatives to thinking of Mao as a fiend who was China's Hitler. One useful way to think of current assessments of Mao is a bit like American views of Andrew Jackson. Though admittedly far from perfect, the comparison is based on the fact that Jackson is remembered both as someone who played a significant role in the development of a political organization (the Democratic Party) that still has many partisans and as someone responsible for brutal policies toward Native Americans that are now often referred to as genocidal.

Both men are thought of as having done terrible things, yet this does not necessarily prevent them from being used as positive symbols. And Jackson still appears on $20 bills, even though Americans now tend to view as heinous the institution of slavery, of which he was a passionate defender, and the early 19th-century military campaigns against Native Americans, in which he took part.

At times Jackson, for all his flaws, is invoked as representing an egalitarian strain within the American democratic tradition, a self-made man of the people who rose to power via straight talk and was not allied with moneyed elitists. Mao stands for something roughly similar. Workers in state-owned industries who in recent years have been laid off understandably associate Mao with a time when laborers got more respect, and he is remembered by some as a Communist leader who, for all his mistakes, never forgot his roots in the countryside and never viewed himself as belonging to a caste that was superior to ordinary folk.

Is Mao seen in China as someone who made errors?

The Chinese population has not been brainwashed into thinking that the Communist Party and its leaders are infallible, and while some people in China still revere Mao as a godlike figure, most do not. There is a widespread acceptance of the fact that Mao made major mistakes. The official verdict, first put forward in the early 1980s, holds that he was 70 percent right and 30 percent wrong. Some Chinese think this too harsh a report card for the leader who made China fully independent of foreign powers for the first time in a century, but others think it far too generous an assessment of him.

Just what his mistakes were is not spelled out in the official account of his legacy. There is a widespread acknowledgement, though, that his biggest missteps came late in life and that, had he died earlier, he might have been seen as right more than 70 percent of the time. It is understood that his most egregious errors included the Great Leap and the Cultural Revolution; with the latter, he is blamed for spurring the Red Guards on to militancy in 1966 and facilitating or at least doing too little to stop the Gang of Four a decade later. When people in China treat him with reverence now, the Mao they have in mind is often the leader of the time before the Great Leap and the Cultural Revolution.

How do ordinary Chinese feel about Mao?

The feelings of ordinary Chinese toward Mao run the gamut from nostalgia to fury, admiration to disdain. There continue to be long lines to view his body, which remains on display in the lavish mausoleum in the center of Tiananmen Square that was built soon after his death. But not everyone who goes to look at him does so in a spirit of reverence (it has long been said that there are those who go just to make sure that the tyrant they feared is really dead, and there are many who go simply as tourists), though some definitely do go to pay homage to a man they still think of as a kind of deity. Most, no doubt, have a mindset not unlike that which citizens of today's France might have when visiting Napoleon's tomb, considering Mao a person of undeniable importance in their country's past, who had his dark side and also made significant contributions to the nation, without which it would not be what it is now.

There are also specific moments when expressing admiration for Mao in contemporary China can serve as a means of criticizing things that have happened since his death. For example, early in the 21st century, angry workers in northern Chinese rust-belt cities who had been laid off from state-run enterprise jobs that Mao had told them would be theirs for life sometimes carried his portrait during their demonstrations as a way of signaling displeasure with economic reforms that were leaving them behind. Mao portraits made another appearance in anti-Japanese protests that took place in the fall of 2012, with commentators suggesting that carrying the likeness of China's former leader served as a way for protestors to express discontent with the direction in which the current leadership was taking the country. China, the presence of the portraits suggested, once again needed a "Great Helmsman" (as Mao had been known) to stand up to the Japanese and settle a territorial dispute between the two countries, as well as steer China back on course more generally.[22]

In addition, there are Chinese who lived through and suffered during the Cultural Revolution who refer to specific things about it—and, by extension, Mao—in a positive way. If annoyed with the self-centeredness and materialism of contemporary youths, they may say that, as bad as the Cultural

Revolution was, having young urbanites experience peasant life firsthand was a good thing.

There are also those who remember Mao in part as the man who achieved important foreign policy goals. For example, they might view positively his role in helping China and North Korea battle the South Korean and United Nations forces to a draw in the 1950s. Or they might view positively Mao's historic 1972 meeting with Richard Nixon, made possible by the fact that the great Chinese modifier of Marxism and the fervently anti-Communist US president shared, by then, an antipathy toward and desire to neutralize the Soviet Union. This paved the way, they know, for the reestablishment of full diplomatic ties between Beijing and Moscow in the late 1970s, when Jimmy Carter was the US president and Deng Xiaoping was China's paramount leader.

Sometimes it is even precisely the qualities of Mao that Jung and Halliday cite as proof of his villainy, such as his alleged inability to feel true affection for his own blood relations, that are turned into positive traits in Chinese criticism of contemporary leaders. For example, when angered by the undue influence wielded and unfair material advantages enjoyed by the princelings of today, some people say that Mao's superiority to his successors is shown by how he treated his progeny. When he sent his son abroad, they note, it was to risk his life alongside his compatriots in war-torn Korea, whereas when Mao's successors send their progeny abroad, it is to study safely ensconced at Oxford University or the Harvard School of Business.

Part II

THE PRESENT AND
THE FUTURE

This half of the book, which focuses on China today and China tomorrow, begins with a chapter called "From Mao to Now," which looks at some of the most significant people (such as Deng Xiaoping), policies (such as the famous, somewhat misleadingly named "One Child Family" drive), and events (including 1989's Tiananmen Uprising and the 2008 Olympics) of the post-Mao or Reform era that began in 1978. One central topic it explores is the surprising longevity of the Chinese Communist Party, an organization that many felt was on its last legs in 1989 and yet was still around to celebrate the PRC's 60th anniversary on October 1, 2009, with a lavish parade featuring everything from floats drawing attention to the special features of each province to displays of the country's latest high-tech weaponry. The second chapter in this section is intended to prepare readers for an era when the United States and China are the world's two superpowers (a period that has just started or soon will, depending on what you think it takes for the PRC to qualify as a true "superpower"). It looks at some of the various ways that the United States has misunderstood and continues to misunderstand China, often because it fails to appreciate just how diverse the PRC is. After that, the chapter then turns the tables to look, more briefly, at Chinese misconceptions about the United States, which often arise from a failure to appreciate how differently the US and Chinese media systems are. The section, and the book, ends with some forecasts about the future and some suggestions about how, in the years to come, the people of the United States and the people of China might begin to see more clearly the big country across the Pacific from them.

4

FROM MAO TO NOW

Who was Deng Xiaoping?

Deng's first revolutionary experiences were as a student in France in the second decade of the 20th century, when he developed a lasting friendship with a fellow radical youth named Zhou Enlai (throughout much of the Mao era, the second-most-important person in China) and became known as "Dr. Mimeograph" because of his role in publicizing progressive causes. For nearly two decades at the end of his eventful life, Deng was the de facto, if not de jure, leader of the PRC. Next to Mao, no one has had as big an impact on the country.

Deng was the architect of the "Reform and Opening" policies that continue to set the course for China's post-Mao economic surge. He was the man who handled the successful negotiations with Margaret Thatcher that smoothed the way for Hong Kong's July 1, 1997, transition from a British territory to a specially administered part of the PRC. (That date was chosen because it marked the end of Britain's ninety-nine-year lease on the land just across the harbor from Hong Kong Island; the British could have tried to keep the island, which was not leased but had been ceded to them outright, but it would have been isolated and would have had difficulty obtaining basic necessities such as water and electricity.) Deng was also the first Chinese Communist leader to move away from a personality-cult approach to leadership. Mao had denied that he wanted such a cult, but then did a great deal to help one develop, and Hua Guofeng continued the tradition. Deng cut it off.

One illustration of this is that Deng's face did not feature prominently on many posters, whereas Mao's had appeared on hundreds (some of which had print runs in the millions), and Hua Guofeng's featured prominently on many posters produced during his short time in power.[1] Similarly, while "Long Live Chairman Mao" and "Long Live Chairman Hua" were common slogans at celebratory state rituals before 1979, in Deng's time and since, the term *wansui* ("long live," literally "ten thousand years") has tended to be used only in calls for the continuation of institutions (the Communist Party), large groups (the people of the PRC), and policies (the unity of all ethnicities). In 1984, at the height of Deng's popularity, some students did hold up a banner saying "Hello Xiaoping" when he reviewed the troops on National Day, and there are some statues honoring him, including a big one in Shenzhen, a city near Hong Kong that he played a key role in transforming from a backwater into a major metropolis, when he made it one of the first "special economic zones," where elements of capitalism are allowed to take root. But, in general, he was seen even at the apex of his authority as the first among equals in an oligarchy rather than as a man who stood completely apart from all other Communist Party leaders.

Throughout the Mao era, Deng was alternately elevated to high posts and demoted in disgrace, sometimes criticized for being too moderate but at other times viewed as having a skill at managing the economy that was invaluable. He was last purged during the Cultural Revolution, when his family also suffered greatly (e.g., one of his sons was bullied to the point of falling off a roof and being crippled for life). And his last rise to prominence came during Hua Guofeng's brief, place-holding stretch as paramount leader.

From late 1978 on, Deng was clearly in charge, and he remained in charge until his death early in 1997 (living not quite long enough to see Hong Kong become part of the PRC). He, however, somewhat mystifyingly, was referred to throughout much of his time in power as simply the nation's "vice-premier" and in his final years was officially "retired," though he still exerted great influence from behind the scenes.

Who were Deng's successors?

One thing that Deng had in common with Mao was an inability to fix upon an heir apparent. As with Mao's chosen successors, those Deng singled out first rose high in the hierarchy and then fell out of favor. This happened to Hu Yaobang (1915–1989), who was elevated to the post of general secretary of the party under Deng but was then demoted to the status of a minor official in 1987 for taking too soft a line against student-led protests. This pattern was repeated with Zhao Ziyang (1919–2005), an important ally to Deng in implementing economic reforms before 1987 and Hu's replacement as general secretary, who was placed under house arrest in 1989 (and stayed there until his death) for taking too soft a line on the Tiananmen Uprising (about which much more below). Deng's final heir apparent was Jiang Zemin (1926–), who took over as general secretary after Zhao's fall.

However, Jiang was not fully in charge until Deng's death. Hu Jintao succeeded Jiang in 2002, but, like Deng in his final years, Jiang continued to be an influential figure despite being officially "retired" and having relinquished most of his formal posts. In November 2012, Hu made a move similar to that of Jiang before him: from a formal holder of power to someone who influences political life, but does so from behind the scenes. Observers of Chinese politics, though, believe that Hu enjoys much less of a support base in the CCP than Jiang does, and it is unlikely that he will exert as much backstage control as Jiang did during Hu's time in power.

It is too early to make definite comments about Jiang's and Hu's eventual posthumous reputations. Both came up with or supported sayings and ideas—the "Three Represents" in Jiang's case, and the call for "Harmonious Society" in Hu's—that they hoped would have the kind of resonance that Deng's "Four Modernizations" and "To Get Rich Is Glorious" had. It seems highly unlikely, though, that historians of the future will look back on those concepts as crucially important. What each is likely to be identified with is the surprisingly smooth power transition of 2002. When Jiang passed the baton to Hu that year, it was the calmest transfer of authority between individuals China had seen in many decades.

The 2002 transition was supposed to set a precedent for future once-every-ten-year hand-offs, but the events of early 2012 underscored just how unusual the 2002 events were. The last year of Hu's time as party secretary got off to a very rocky start, as Bo Xilai, a leading contender for a position on the Standing Committee, was purged amid a murder scandal (about which more below). The 18th Party Congress, which most observers anticipated would be held in September or early October, did not take place until November, allegedly because of back-room squabbles among the party elite over which officials would be elevated to the powerful Politburo Standing Committee. When it did finally take place, though, it went smoothly, with no major last-minute surprises. The Standing Committee's size was reduced from nine members to seven, but that was expected. Many observers thought Hu would retain his military posts for a brief period after ceding his civilian ones, as Jiang had done before him, but instead these passed immediately to Xi. And Jiang was more of a public presence during the transition than some predicted he would be, which led to discussion of the continued strength of factions linked to him. None of these events, however, equaled the drama surrounding the Bo Xilai case that preceded the actual convening of the Congress.

What exactly did Deng do?

Deng Xiaoping's main foreign policy accomplishment, aside from brokering the deal over Hong Kong, was to normalize relations with Washington. As the first PRC leader to travel to the United States, in 1979, he was seen in Washington early on as the only head of a communist party with whom the United States could easily do business. He was responsible as well for the reestablishment of regular relations between Moscow and Beijing in the 1980s. One reason that the Tiananmen protests received such widespread international media coverage, in fact, was that when the protests began, Mikhail Gorbachev was in China taking part in a series of high-profile meetings with Deng that were supposed to cement the restoration of close ties between the world's two largest Communist states.

When Deng is remembered positively, however, it is above all not for what he did on the international front (where he was not always successful: a brief but costly war with Vietnam occurred under his watch at the end of the 1970s), but rather for his introducing a series of bold economic reforms that paved the way for China's two decades of record-breaking growth. These reforms were intended to temper Communist ideology with limited forms of private entrepreneurship, appeals for foreign investment, and a partial reduction of state control over agriculture and industry. The goal was to unleash pent-up entrepreneurial energy, revitalize farming by allowing the most productive farmers to sell some of their yield for profit, and promote "Socialism with Chinese Characteristics," a unique economic system in which the state would still control much of the economy but that would allow greater room for free enterprise and decentralization than there had been in the era of Soviet-style five-year plans.

How is Deng viewed now?

Had he died before 1989, Deng would have gone down in history in both the West and in China as a celebrated figure. He was admired for his pragmatism (in contrast to Mao, who emphasized ideological purity, Deng claimed he didn't care if a cat was a "black cat or a white cat" because if it caught mice, it was a "good cat") and for slogans that moved away from a focus on class struggle ("To Get Rich Is Glorious" was another of his best-known slogans). He was selected as *Time* magazine's "Person of the Year" not once but twice, in 1978 and 1985. Only one previous Chinese leader, Chiang Kai-shek, who had been a personal favorite of Time-Life's chief, Henry Luce, had been given that honor even once—and when he had been singled out for it, he had to share it with his spouse, the only time that a "Man and Wife of the Year" were recognized by *Time*. Though there were many parts of Deng's policies that stopped short of representing a full embrace of capitalism, he was often described as creating a China that was more capitalist than Communist.

Currently, though Deng is officially venerated in China as a man who did great things for the nation, his international reputation is mixed. While he is associated with economic reforms that paved the way for China's transformation from a Third World economy to the world's third economy, he is also associated with a go-slow approach to political reforms, a man who elevated China's GDP and place in the world but crushed dissident movements, including the Democracy Wall protests of the late 1970s and, even more importantly, the Tiananmen Uprising. When an American academic published a sympathetic biography of Deng in 2011, many reviewers criticized the book's author for being far too kind to the late leader. Others acknowledged that Deng, like Mao, remains a complicated figure whose legacy is impossible to summarize in a single sound bite.[2]

What was the Democracy Wall movement?

The Democracy Wall movement was named for the place in Beijing where protesters began to put up manifestos, poems, and other documents of dissent in the fall of 1978. The aims and rhetoric of the activists varied widely, as many were inspired by Marxist ideas or at least by critical strains within the Communist world (e.g., Yugoslavian reformist calls for a check on the tendency for cadres to become an elitist "new class" within state socialist settings), while others were influenced by liberal concepts. The *minzhu* in the 1970s' *minzhuqiang* (meaning "democracy wall," a term first used for a protest space in the late 1940s and then used in the same way during the Hundred Flowers period of the late 1950s) could, in other words, stand for many things, but primarily it expressed a desire for rulers more prepared to listen to the people sound their concerns.

At first, Deng seemed to think that it was a good thing that people were venting their hopes and frustrations. By the end of 1979, however, in a sort of replay of the Hundred Flowers campaign's conclusion, the government labeled the protests dangerous and imprisoned some of the boldest authors of posters.

The best-known Democracy Wall participant is Wei Jingsheng (1950–), who was imprisoned for many years for his activism and now lives in the United States as a political exile. His famous poster played upon Deng's policy of the "Four Modernizations," which emphasized the need for China to modernize work in the realms of agriculture, industry, technology, and defense. China also needed, Wei insisted, a "Fifth Modernization" (the name of his manifesto): democratic reform.

What is the real story of the Tiananmen Uprising?

Most Westerners over forty, though they may know little about the Democracy Wall movement, believe they understand the major facts of the Tiananmen Uprising, especially if they followed the drama in real time on television. And many Westerners younger than that think they know at least the basic outline of the course of events.

Yet, in many instances, the details have become scrambled in Western memory, with the complex story of Tiananmen reduced to a stand-off between a male "student"—though the man in question was probably a worker—and a line of tanks. A major source of confusion concerns who exactly died in the June 4th Massacre (more about that below); how these victims were killed (Westerners often assume most were crushed by tanks, but automatic weapons caused many more deaths); and where they were slain (not in Tiananmen Square, hence my avoidance of the term "Tiananmen Square Massacre," but in the streets near that giant plaza).

The Chinese government continues to insist that there was no massacre at all. They maintain instead that the event was simply an effort by soldiers—who showed great restraint when dealing with crowds, and sometimes lost their lives in the process—to put an end to a "counterrevolutionary riot" that disrupted life in China's capital, threatened the stability of the nation, and, if left unchecked, could have sent the country spiraling into the kind of disorder that had characterized the Cultural Revolution era.

That view of events has been labeled in the West, quite appropriately, the "Big Lie" about 1989. A few soldiers were killed, but they were not the only, or even the main, victims of the violence of early June. The government exaggerated greatly when raising the bogeyman of the Cultural Revolution, given that the protests of 1989 were largely nonviolent.

The Big Lie is not, however, the only widely but incorrectly disseminated version of key events. For example, many in the West continue to believe, erroneously, that most or all of those killed during the June 4th Massacre were students. In fact, most were members of other classes. They also continue to believe that the main slogans protesters rallied to in 1989 were calls for "democracy," when in reality there was much more emphasis at the time on the evils of corruption than on a desire for elections.

Students did take the lead in the initial protests, and one of their goals was to push for political reform. The Tiananmen Uprising was a sequel of sorts to an earlier wave of campus protests, which were, like those of 1989, rooted in a complex mix of frustrations and desires. The youths involved wanted more personal freedom and were frustrated with various aspects of university life, from compulsory calisthenics to the low quality of cafeteria food, and they wanted campus leaders to be chosen via open elections rather than being handpicked by the party. These protests swept through several Chinese cities in December 1986 (the biggest demonstrations occurred in Shanghai) and ended at the start of 1987 (with Beijing students making a New Year's Day march to Tiananmen Square).

There were some scattered protests in 1988, but the resurgence of a true movement did not come until April 1989. There were plans in the works for a demonstration on May 4, when the 80th anniversary of China's greatest student movement arrived, but a fluke event jump-started the struggle. This event was the mid-April death of Hu Yaobang, who had become a hero to the students when he was criticized and demoted for taking a soft line on the 1986–1987 protests.

Hu's death opened a window of opportunity for the students: when Hu died, he was still an official, albeit not a high-ranking one, so the state could hardly prevent people from gathering to mourn his passing. The students turned the occasion into an act of protest in addition to an expression of sadness when they began remarking what a shame it was when good men died, while bad ones lived on and stayed in control.

One key difference from the 1986–1987 protests was that, by the time the Tiananmen Uprising had peaked in May, it was much more than just a student movement. By then, the most important demonstrations involved members of many different social groups. Workers were particularly numerous in marches, drawn to the cause partly by the fact that, though students made democracy one of their watchwords, they spent as much energy attacking the leadership for growing corrupt and failing to spread the fruits of economic development broadly enough. This criticism echoed powerfully throughout Chinese society at a time when inflation was rampant and it often seemed that the only people growing rich were the children of top leaders and those with high-level official connections.

Support from other classes peaked after students staged a hunger strike, an act that had special potency since lavish banquets had become a symbol of officials' selfish behavior. Tapping into a longstanding Chinese tradition of educated youths laying their bodies on the line to protect the nation, the hunger strikers were seen by many as having proved that they were far more deeply committed to the good of the country than were Deng and other party oligarchs.

Given the cross-class makeup of the crowds at the biggest marches—tens or hundreds of thousands of people took to the streets and central squares of cities such as Shanghai and Guangzhou, while a million rallied in Beijing—it should not come as a shock to learn that the majority of the hundreds of people killed in early June (there is no official death toll, but that seems the likely size of it) were not students. Some students died, but the majority of those slain, both in Beijing and in the western city of Chengdu, where a massacre also occurred in early June, were workers and other ordinary city dwellers.[3]

Why hasn't the Chinese government changed its line on Tiananmen?

Many supporters of the Tiananmen movement hoped that, within a few years, the regime would reassess the protests of 1989. A similar set of 1976 demonstrations, which also centered on Tiananmen Square and which were also triggered in part by the death of an admired official—in that case, Zhou Enlai—were initially dubbed "counterrevolutionary riots" but then, after Deng's rise, reassessed as a "patriotic" struggle. Relatives of slain students and workers, and human rights activists around the world, have pushed for a similar reassessment of the protests of 1989, but this has not come to pass.

One reason is that there has not been the kind of dramatic shift within the party leadership as occurred in the aftermath of the 1976 protests. Deng's 1978 rise signaled a dramatic turnaround, and he could logically interpret the 1976 protests as a precocious signal of support for his eventual assumption of power.

The situation relating to the June 4th Massacre is very different. There are various kinds of tensions within China's current leadership group, including ones between those linked to Jiang Zemin and those with closer ties to Hu Jintao (who in 1989 was a high-ranking official in Tibet, an area that also saw unrest that year). But all the main patrons of current leaders, and many of the leaders themselves, were closely associated with Deng and his policies and see themselves as continuing the reforms he started. They resist taking actions that could be regarded as repudiating Deng's vision for fear that doing so might, by extension, serve to undermine their own legitimacy.

What effect did the fall of other Communist governments have on China?

It would be easy to assume that the international climate during the last years of the previous century and the first years of this one was not conducive to regimes that are linked to the ideas of Karl Marx. This is debatable: some have claimed that the events of 1989 proved Marx wrong, once and for all, but others, including some at the center or on the right of the political spectrum, have claimed to have been struck, upon reading or rereading texts such as "The Communist Manifesto," by Marx's ideas about what we now call globalization.[4] Whatever the case may be, recent trends in world affairs, even if bad for

Marxism per se, have made it easier for the CCP to defend its distinctive current version of this creed.

Consider, for example, how well events of the 1990s fit in with the regime's assertion that China's national interest was best served by a strong state and emphasis on stability as something to be valued. For Beijing propagandists trying to argue for this point of view, the Yugoslavian descent into chaos was a godsend.

The collapse of order in that part of southeastern Europe allowed the CCP to point out, if not in these precise terms, that no matter how dissatisfied someone might be to live in a *Communist* state, there was a less appealing alternative out there: living in a *post-Communist* country such as those in the unstable and war-torn region that Tito had once governed. Furthermore, after NATO forces intervened to protect Kosovo, the CCP was able to claim that a post-Communist era involved not just economic collapse and widespread violence but also a loss of independence—an especially sore point in a nation that long suffered from imperialist encroachments.

The year 1989 presented a major challenge to the CCP that many thought it only barely managed to withstand: the protest wave that brought a million people into the streets of Beijing and onto the capital's biggest plaza and drew tens or hundreds of thousands into the central districts of scores of other cities. The party survived, but only, as we have seen, after Deng Xiaoping and the other oligarchs of his generation took a series of drastic steps. Specifically, they ordered the June 4th Massacre (*liusi*, or 6/4, remains the most common Chinese term for the events of 1989), they carried out a campaign of mass arrests, and they demoted Zhao Ziyang and placed him under house arrest. The other key event of 1989 was the rise to power of Jiang Zemin, the Shanghai leader who proved his skills to the oligarchs by taking a firm stand against the protests and restoring order in his city using only limited force.

The year was also a challenging one for Deng and his allies because Communist regimes fell in Budapest, Bucharest, and other European capitals. In 1989, Solidarity rose to power in Poland (winning its first election on the very day that PLA soldiers were firing into crowds in Beijing), the Velvet Revolution occurred in Prague, and the Berlin Wall crumbled. And though the Soviet Union remained intact and under Communist Party rule, its days seemed numbered.

In the wake of these developments, it became the conventional wisdom outside of China that the group responsible for the June 4th brutality could not possibly hold on to power for long. The catchphrase was that the "End of History" had arrived and soon there would be no Communist states left. Throughout the 1990s, the notion that the CCP was unlikely to endure remained an article of faith for many Western journalists, academics, and policymakers, though there began to be more and more dissenting voices during the first years of the new century, as it became doubtful that the "Leninist extinction" (another phrase from the Western literature of the time) would affect Beijing.[5]

The tide has shifted even more recently. Many now agree that, barring unexpected events, the CCP is likely to be with us for some time to come. In fact, it can now claim, playing on a famous phrase attributed to Mark Twain, that reports of its death have been greatly exaggerated—and Communist Party leaders might not mind being linked to a line associated with that particular American author, given that he was a sharp critic of US imperialism and even wrote an editorial early in his career calling attention to the unfairness of the treaty-port system.

How did China's rulers avoid falling prey to the "Leninist extinction"?

One reason that Deng and Jiang were able to prove the skeptics wrong in the 1990s has already been noted: they have been able to point to the traumas experienced by some formerly Communist countries. Their 21st-century successors have continued to do this, while also making corollary efforts to highlight and amplify any bad news relating to non-Communist countries where dictators or authoritarian groups have been overthrown. The Chinese state media made a great deal, for example, of how chaotic, dangerous, and strife-ridden Iraq became after Saddam Hussein was toppled. Here are four other factors worth stressing when seeking to understand the surprising longevity of the CCP.

First, the regime has made great and largely successful efforts to co-opt traditionally restive or particularly troublesome groups. Entrepreneurs who were frustrated by getting too little respect from the authorities and having too little influence in how China was run were among those who supported the 1989 protests and are now welcomed into the Communist Party. Intellectuals in post-1989 China have access to a much wider array of books and journal articles and can travel abroad more easily, and this has helped minimize, though not completely eradicate, their disaffection with the party, which led so many of them to support the Tiananmen protests. And the government has stopped micromanaging daily life on university campuses, which has similarly lessened the discontent of students, whose actions were crucial in 1989.

Second, the regime has followed a post-1989 strategy of patriotic education, emphasizing the party's historical ties to anti-imperialist movements. Like all of the other enduring Communist Party regimes (those of North Korea, Vietnam, and Cuba) and unlike many of those that fell in 1989 (including those in Poland and Hungary), China's came to power via an independence struggle.

Also like the heads of those other regimes, China's leaders make overstated claims about the role their organization played in saving their country from imperialists and underplay the contributions of other groups, but all the Communist organizations still in power are justified in asserting ties to nationalist risings. In the Chinese case, the party's role in anti-Japanese resistance battles is celebrated whenever the regime's legitimacy needs burnishing, and China's role in the Korean War (presented as an effort to free a neighboring government from foreign domination) is also commemorated.[6]

Third, the regime has worked hard to dramatically raise the standard of living and availability of consumer goods within its leading cities. This is something that none of the Communist Party regimes that fell late in the last century managed to do, and that failure helped bring about the collapse of those ruling groups. Purely political concerns, including frustration relating to issues of freedom of speech, contributed to dissatisfaction with the Communist regimes that fell in 1989, as did a sense, in many cases, that these governments were foreign impositions (stooges of Moscow), but material issues contributed, too. People living in East Berlin, for example, knew that on the other side of the Berlin Wall, in what had formerly been part of the same city, one could shop at much more attractive department stores and supermarkets. Comparable things could have been said in 1989 about the contrast between Shanghai and capitalist Taipei in Taiwan, but the difference is now gone. Europe's state socialist regimes claimed that they not only were morally superior to their capitalist rivals but also could compete with them materially. They could not, and it cost them. China's leadership has done a better job at quite literally delivering the goods.

Fourth, the regime has adopted a flexible strategy toward new protests that has worked well to prevent a new broad-based movement from taking shape. Mao famously said that a single spark could turn into a prairie fire. And China's leaders certainly do not govern a country where conflagrations are uncommon, since there are, by their own admission, tens of thousands of protests every year. They have thus far managed, however, by using different measures to deal with different sorts of unrest, to keep these many sparks from igniting another nationwide blaze.

How has the government responded to protests since 1989?

The authorities have used harsh measures to suppress some kinds of unrest and gone to extraordinary lengths to limit awareness of these actions. But it has taken a less draconian stance toward other sorts of resistance, at times even punishing local officials who have been criticized by protesters.[7] This point deserves close scrutiny, since the Western press gives so much attention to patterns of dissent and moments of upheaval in the PRC, and because the mix of factors that determines how exactly the government responds to a particular protest is far from straightforward.

The calculus that tips the official response toward or away from outright repression is complex. Equally complicated is the decision about whether there will be a complete or merely partial effort to block information about what has occurred. Because of what happened during the Tiananmen Uprising and an awareness of the importance of cross-class protests in places such as Poland in the 1980s, movements involving members of more than one occupational or economic group are seen as particularly dangerous. Also key is how geographically dispersed dissenters are: purely local events—ranging from small-scale tax strikes to neighborhood discussions of new chemical plants—tend to be treated more leniently. A third factor that influences the severity of the regime's response, both toward protesters and toward domestic and foreign journalists seeking to cover events, is how well organized dissenters seem to be. The less evidence of careful coordination, the more likely the response will be to mollify crowds, rather than strike terror into them—and the more likely reporters will be allowed to cover the event.

For example, when the Arab Spring protest movement broke out in early 2011, the PRC government moved swiftly to ensure that nothing similar would take place in China. Though there was little sign that any "Jasmine" protests were even planned, authorities initiated a widespread Internet crack-down and arrested a number of human rights lawyers and activists, including the prominent artist Ai Weiwei. Chinese leaders apparently feared the threat of a wide-ranging protest movement that could appeal to many different social groups and spark a repeat of the Tiananmen Uprising.

Later in 2011, however, events in the Guangdong province village of Wukan provided an example of how local protests can sometimes garner government approval, rather than cen-sure. Wukan residents complained that their local Communist Party representatives were illegally seizing and selling vil-lagers' land without providing fair compensation. One of the leading protestors then died under mysterious circumstances while in police custody, further escalating tensions, and vil-lagers soon drove the party cadres out of town. Guangdong authorities initially blockaded Wukan and surrounded the village with security forces. But they soon began negotiat-ing with the villagers and eventually reached a settlement: Wukan residents would be allowed to elect a new village party chief and the stand-off between the province and pro-testors would end.

Three additional facts are worth noting. First, geography helps determine whether a hard or soft line will be taken. Force definitely tends to be used much more swiftly when unrest occurs in frontier zones, such as Tibet and Xinjiang, where large percentages of the population do not belong to the majority Han group, and where economic grievances and anger associated with ethnic and religious divides make for a particularly volatile combination.

Second, the regime's relatively lenient treatment of some protests can be interpreted as a sign of self-confidence. The political scientist Kevin O'Brien has made a strong case that it is a mistake to treat reports that many protests occur as indi-cators of weakness. It may be a sign of regime strength that the government is ready, not just to admit that protests are occurring, but sometimes even to allow people to let off steam without responding harshly.[8]

Finally, it seems that protestors in China have the greatest chance of achieving their objectives if they point out that what they seek is simply for the party to fulfill the concrete promises it has made to its citizens. Disputes over fair compensation for land taken by the government, for example, appear likely to be resolved relatively smoothly, as in Wukan. On the other hand, those who pursue bigger, more abstract goals—such as democracy or religious freedom—more frequently find themselves arrested and tried on charges of "inciting subversion of state power."

Why and how has the CCP suppressed the Falun Gong movement?

A campaign of repression that has particularly baffled foreign observers is that which the regime quickly undertook to crush the Falun Gong sect just over a decade ago; likewise, the resoluteness of China's policy toward the group since the suppression perplexes foreigners. When the crackdown began, the group in question had never engaged in a violent protest, and it seemed—to outsiders at least—to be simply a spiritual movement, chiefly involving the practice of meditation and gentle exercises known as *qigong*. Led by a man named Li Hongzhi—whose admittedly unusual ideas include claims to powers that many Westerners would consider akin to magical, and a version of "scientific facts" many would dub superstitions—the Falun Gong nonetheless did not have a political agenda. The fact that the Chinese government viewed the Falun Gong as a threat is easy to understand, however, using the rubric outlined above. That is, the threat derived from its adherents' coming from all walks of life (even some CCP officials had joined it), being popular throughout the country (cells formed in many cities), and showing a capability for coordinated action. This capability manifest itself in April 1999, when ten thousand protesters assembled outside the Beijing compound where China's highest leaders live and staged a sit-in demanding an end to official criticism of the group.

Other reasons have been given for the ruthless campaign against Falun Gong. A leading scholar of the subject, the historian David Ownby, stresses the ideological challenge that the Falun Gong posed to the CCP even before it began to present the party as an evil organization (something that occurred after the crackdown against its members began). Ownby convincingly argues that the CCP was threatened by Li's novel fusion of Chinese traditions and modern "science," for the party claims a monopoly on bringing together what it means to be both Chinese and modern via the "scientific" socialism of Marx.[9]

The CCP response to the Falun Gong needs to be seen as a special case for other reasons as well. For example, during imperial times, Chinese regimes were sometimes weakened or overthrown by millenarian religious movements, including some that began as quiescent self-help sects. And the party is especially concerned about protests that have ties with charismatic figures, of whom Li would surely be one. That said, the CCP response still illustrates the general pattern described above of struggles being treated as most serious when they are multiclass, geographically widespread, and organized.

Who are the Chinese dissidents now?

One common mistake that Americans, and some other foreigners, no doubt, make is to assume that in China one is either a dissident (who boldly challenges the government and ends up in prison or in exile) or a loyalist (who follows the regime's line, whether out of belief or fear). In fact, however, there have always been and definitely still are many people in the middle.

On the extreme loyalist end of the spectrum, there are those who make their careers doing work designed to shore up and promote the policies of China's current leaders. And on the opposite end are those who openly confront the authorities and at times, such as when they form opposition parties, seem to be daring the state to take steps to silence them. But most Chinese fall somewhere between these extremes. Lingering Cold War assumptions tempt one to assume that there are no "critical intellectuals" in state socialist countries, but in China they certainly exist. They do not directly challenge the authority of the CCP yet do criticize aspects of the established order.

Many artists and writers operate in a "gray zone," where they bend or even flout the rules to evade the PRC's censorship mechanisms, but do not confront the government outright. Instead, they make careful judgment calls about how far they can push before the authorities will push back. Authors, especially, are taking advantage of the power of the Internet, which allows them to disseminate writings without going through official publishing channels. And some, like novelist and essayist Yu Hua (1960–), publish their more controversial works in Hong Kong and Taiwan, or arrange for English-language versions of their most challenging pieces to appear in foreign publications, thus remaining free to live on the mainland.[10]

There are also activist lawyers who generally work within the system, yet take up cases by people struggling to call attention to specific abuses by local officials. And there are members of various single-issue NGOs who publicize what they see as flawed government policies relating to topics such as AIDS or the environment, yet do not advocate any kind of radical change in government. One example is the self-taught blind lawyer Chen Guangcheng (1971–), who has filed lawsuits and organized opposition to forced abortions and other extreme methods of enforcing China's One-Child Policy. Chen was jailed from 2006 to 2010, then placed under house arrest until April 2012, when he escaped and fled to the US embassy in Beijing. Though the Chinese government eventually allowed him to leave China and enroll as a special student at New York

University's law school, Chen has maintained that he hopes to return to China and continue his work there.

Someone who might fit into the more conventional Western image of a dissident is avant-garde artist Ai Weiwei (1957–), who lived in New York for over a decade before returning to China in 1993 and who seems to delight in provoking the Chinese government. At one point, Ai was an artistic consultant on the "Bird's Nest" stadium constructed for the Beijing Olympics, but he then turned against the project and denounced the Games as propaganda for the CCP. Ai attracted the most government displeasure, though, when he began investigating the deaths of over five thousand schoolchildren who perished as a result of poorly constructed schools that collapsed in the 2008 Sichuan earthquake. Ai listed the children's names on his blog, which was then shut down by the authorities. In the spring of 2011, security forces arrested Ai and held him for alleged "economic crimes." (He was later charged with income tax evasion.) Detained for over two months, Ai was then permitted to return to his Beijing home, though he remains under surveillance and cannot leave the country.

When Mo Yan (1955–) was given the Nobel Prize in Literature in 2012, some commentators used the contrast between his career and Ai's to chide the Swedish judges for making a foolish choice. Whereas Ai's art challenged the state, they claimed, Mo's supported it. Whereas Ai was censored and bullied, Mo was lauded and served as a vice chairman of the official Writer's Association. There are crucial differences between the two, which Mo himself underscored in some of the statements he made after winning the prize, claiming in one that censorship could benefit rather than harm artists. It is also worth noting, though, that some of Mo's writings have veered at least tentatively into the "gray zone," if not as daringly as those of Yu Hua (a member, though not a vice chairman, of the Writer's Association). Mo is no "dissident," but his writings are not devoid of elements of social critique. He can be caustic about the corrosive effects of government corruption on communities, albeit taking aim at local officials only—a far safer target than national ones.[11] Mo has stayed far enough inside the confines of the safe zone to be celebrated by the Chinese leadership for his Nobel Prize, a story very different from that of the PRC's previous Nobel Prize winner, Liu Xiaobo.

Who is Liu Xiaobo?

Liu Xiaobo (1955–) had been an activist in China for two decades before many in the West ever heard his name, when he was awarded the Nobel Peace Prize in 2010. In the 1980s, Liu was a rising star in academia, renowned for his path-breaking work on literary criticism. His academic career came to an end, though, when Liu joined the Tiananmen protests and emerged as one of the leaders of the moderate faction that wanted to leave the square peacefully. Liu was arrested soon after the June 4th Massacre and imprisoned for almost two years. Resuming his work as an outspoken political activist and writer upon his release, Liu has repeatedly been detained and placed under house arrest. On December 25, 2009, he was sentenced to an eleven-year term for "inciting subversion of state power," a charge brought about by his role in composing "Charter 08" the year before. Liu and other dissidents took the inspiration for this document from Václav Havel's "Charter 77"; they asked the government for democratic reforms, an independent judiciary, and freedom of expression. Circulated online, the petition received thousands of signatures.

Liu was the first PRC citizen to win a Nobel Prize, but the Chinese government expressed no joy at the news. Authorities denounced the award and relations between China and Norway grew chilly (though the Nobel committee is an independent organization not under the control of the Norwegian government). Nineteen countries with ties to China—including Russia, Cuba, Iraq, and Venezuela—boycotted the award ceremony in Oslo, and the PRC prevented Liu's wife and friends from attending the event on his behalf by refusing to let them exit the country. After the chairman of the prize committee read the citation honoring Liu, the audience gave an extended standing ovation to the empty chair where Liu was meant to have sat.[12]

What is the role of the Internet in political dissent?

It would be easy to imagine that the Chinese Internet is a hotbed of political dissent, particularly since the government sometimes seems preoccupied with silencing (often in a clumsy fashion) discordant voices. But for many—perhaps even most—young Chinese, the Internet is simply an entertainment outlet: a place where they can chat with friends, make purchases, and play games late into the night (leading to a number of articles in the press about the dangers of Internet addiction). And while there are a few prominent outspoken bloggers, such as the racecar driver and writer Han Han (1982–), who might be the most widely read blogger in the world, many others are not interested in promoting political change. Yet they remain passionate about being able to express their opinions about topics that interest them and to follow stories that strike them as important.[13]

One venue where critical voices do tend to proliferate and attract censure from the authorities is the Twitter-like microblogging platforms called Weibo. Users often post stories of corruption and official malfeasance, which censors rush to take down from the site before the posts can be picked up by others. Despite the rumored tens of thousands of censors the government employs, however, removing Weibo posts is much like playing a game of Whac-A-Mole: as quickly as the content is deleted in one location, it pops up in another. And though censors can block particular terms on Weibo sites, users are adept at finding innocuous homophones (using different written characters) to evade those blocks. It might appear, then, that a Weibo poster is complaining about his dislike of river crabs (*hexie*), but savvy readers will understand that his real target is the "Harmonious Society" (*hexie shehui*) program that Hu Jintao made his signature effort while he was China's president.

What does the digital divide mean in China?

It has become common to refer to the existence of a "digital divide" that separates those who use the web from those who do not. The digital divide persists in most of the world, of course, and is further characterized by some people having their own laptop and fast Internet access, for example, whereas others can use the Internet only at a cybercafé, and still others have only occasional access to a computer with a slow connection.

In China, however, there is another level of distinction due to the government's sophisticated censorship mechanisms, which some refer to as constituting "the Great Firewall of China" and others describe as the working of the "Net Nanny." These tools strive to make some sites inaccessible and to ensure that searches for sensitive terms yield either no results or only links that provide government-sanctioned information.

A search for the term "June 4" will likely retrieve no results at all, for example, and a search for "Tiananmen" will deliver links to official sites devoted to the square but not point the searcher to overseas sites containing student manifestos issued at Tiananmen in 1989. There are, however, ways to circumvent the "Great Firewall" and frustrate the Net Nanny's plans; these involve proxy servers and VPNs—tools that, in a sense, make it seem as though a computer located in China is actually based somewhere else. This creates another divide among Internet users in China, separating those who are versed in using such techniques from those who are not.

Still another divide, which is less absolute, is between what could be called critical and noncritical users of the web. There are those who do not think much about the nature of information provided online and whether it reinforces or challenges official viewpoints. There are also, though, some readers and writers who access the mainland's controlled web largely, though not exclusively, with an eye toward conveying or consuming alternative views of current affairs. They take pride in posting provocative comments that can stay online at least temporarily due to clever forms of wording, from using "river crab" to refer to "harmony" to using the Chinese terms for the imaginary date of "May 35th" to allude to June 4th, a date that is taboo in Chinese media since it was when the 1989 massacre took place. Han Han is a master at crafting enigmatic, satiric, or allegorical posts that are able to stay up at least briefly because censors are not sure what to make of them. When Liu Xiaobo received the Nobel Prize, for example, Han Han's blog simply carried a pair of quotation marks with nothing between them, something that many readers eventually concluded meant that he had much he wanted to say, but that none of it would be allowed. And in another post, which might put an American reader in mind of a Stephen Colbert faux polemic, he extolled the virtues of the controversial Three Gorges Dam in a way that made it clear to savvy readers that he was actually deeply concerned about its environmental impact and other problems.

For every Han Han and related writer, there are millions of Chinese Internet readers who may not engage in word play or veiled political commentary themselves, but enjoy finding it online. This helps explain Han Han's enormous popularity, though his celebrity status as a successful rally driver and novelist and his good looks—all of which keep him on magazine covers—play a part as well. When his blog posts get wiped off the web, like scrubbed-out Weibo messages, they often live on via being placed on other sites. This reposting, which may be done by people who never or rarely blog themselves, blurs the line between producers and consumers of challenging online content.

Is the Great Firewall of China
a unique structure?

The Chinese government's Internet policies, like its policies in frontier zones such as Xinjiang, can cause one to overstate the distinctiveness of the PRC. Contributing to a vision of uniqueness in this case is nomenclature. The term "Great Firewall of China" is a clever one. It offers a nice rhetorical twist on the country's best-known landmark. And it is not only Western commentators who use it; many Chinese bloggers who try to circumvent the censors have had fun with the phrase as well—so much so that references to and images of "wall climbers" became very popular in Chinese cyberspace in 2009.[14] And yet, we are led astray if we allow the term to fool us into thinking that what the Chinese government is doing vis-à-vis the Internet has no foreign parallels.

In fact, many regimes strive to limit the kinds of materials that can be accessed online within the territories they govern. The Iranian government is a case in point. Similarities between Chinese and Iranian bloggers had been noted before, but the China–Iran Internet control analogies became particularly clear in June 2009. The month opened with Beijing officials trying to limit online discussion of the 20th anniversary of the 1989 protests and ended with their counterparts in Tehran clamping down on social media such as Twitter and generally employing related strategies—though in a less sophisticated and slower manner than the Chinese authorities—in a largely unsuccessful effort to curtail the spread of information about a popular movement.[15]

Nonauthoritarian regimes also seek to control what is said online, limiting certain kinds of communications (often those deemed "pornographic"). Some of the precise measures that the Chinese regime uses to defang the Internet are distinctive, but Beijing's leaders are not in a class all their own. This is why I prefer the term "Net Nanny," which encourages us to think of the PRC as one of a variety of places (along with Singapore and Saudi Arabia, for example) in which a good deal of energy is spent trying to get Internet users to go to preferred sites and to steer clear of what the state deems "harmful" modes of online behavior.[16]

Why were the 2008 Olympics such a big deal for China?

Large-scale spectacles, including the National Day parades held on October 1 every ten years (most recently in 2009), have long played important roles in the political life of the PRC. Recently, the government has emphasized hosting high-profile international gatherings, from summits to film festivals to large-scale sporting events, that bring people from around the world to China. The Beijing Games were the biggest spectacle of this kind ever held in the PRC.

The government greeted with enthusiasm the news in 2001 that the Chinese bid for the 2008 Games had been accepted. There was a great deal of popular excitement about the Games, too, as many Chinese were well aware that the Olympics are now the most attention-grabbing mega-event in the world, one that gives considerable prestige to countries chosen to host the Summer Games in particular.

At the same time, people were not always happy with the preparations necessary to stage the Games. For example, the Olympics-related building boom required many long-term Beijing residents to relocate to less central districts. When residents felt that the compensation offered was appropriate and replacement accommodations an improvement, they made the move willingly. But some felt that the deals offered were too stingy or were distressed at having to abandon neighborhood ties and memory-filled haunts. Developers were often accused of bullying tactics and taking unfair advantage of official connections. Beijing also went to unusual lengths to upgrade its ground transportation system and built a completely new state-of-the-art airport.

What does the handling of
the Beijing Games say about today's China?

The unusually elaborate preparations for the Beijing Games and other international events, including the 2010 Shanghai World Expo, touted as an "Economic Olympics," suggest that there is an unusual intensity to China's concern with mega-events. But it has been common for countries that are rising rapidly in global hierarchies to start hosting both Olympics and World's Fair–like spectacles, something that the United States did between 1876 (the year of the Philadelphia Centennial Exhibition, the first North American World's Fair) and the early 1900s (when the country began playing host to the Games).

The most important general point about World's Fairs (formerly the dominant international mega-events) and the Summer Olympics (the spectacle that currently holds that distinction, due partly to the rise of television and the way they lend themselves to visual media coverage) is that they often have the effect of symbolically dividing countries into different categories, according to the degree of economic development, military might, integration into the global order, or some combination of these three things—with those seen as able to host major mega-events placed at the top of the heap.

It is no mere coincidence that when World's Fairs were dominant, they were often staged in Western European cities that were the capitals of major empires. Paris hosted four between 1855 and 1900, while London hosted two of the first three ever staged. It is also no coincidence that several of the first major international exhibitions outside of Europe were held in the United States, when the United States was rapidly industrializing, becoming much more urban, and beginning to assert itself forcefully on the global stage—as China is now.

In China, the country's dream to become the kind that can host an Olympics dates to the early 1900s, and so, too, does the country's dream to someday host a World's Fair (a 1902 science fiction story by a famous Chinese intellectual imagined an international exhibition in Shanghai in the then far-off year of 1962). Also dating back to that time is China's dream to become the kind of country that could produce athletes who would win medals at the Games.

The significance of this last dream was intimately tied to a political concern: a desire to shed the nation's global reputation as the "sick man of Asia" (a phrase that resonates with the Ottoman Empire's earlier nickname, the "sick man of Europe"). This vision of Chinese weakness, which followed the Qing defeats at the hands of, first, militarily superior Western powers and then Japan, was one that nationalists of all political stripes were eager to shed.

The emphasis that both Mao and Chiang Kai-shek placed on physical education in their early writings, and the public displays of stamina that the former exhibited later in life (such as his famous swims in the Yangzi River), is relevant here as well. The quest for Olympic glory, both in terms of winning numerous medal counts and the Games, can thus be seen in part as an expression of China's desire to put behind it once and for all any lingering sense that it is a weak country.

Will grand spectacles continue to be important to China?

Post-Olympic China has continued to be and will likely remain a country that regularly holds grand spectacles. Some have raised the possibility that China will seek to hold another Olympics within the next few decades. There is also talk of trying to mount a Chinese bid for the athletic event that is currently second only in global import to the Olympics: the FIFA World Cup.

Mega-events of this sort, which are sponsored by international organizations, play a role in confirming a vision, based partly on official myth but also partly in tangible reality, that China is a once powerful country that was laid low for a time and has now risen again to a more natural status. They show that China has gone from being the kind of country that could only play minor roles in the great World's Fairs of the 1800s (in which it was treated as a "backward" country that should display "exotic" aspects of its culture rather than a "modern" one that should display its latest machines and canons) to being the kind that can host 21st-century counterparts to those attention-getting and status-conveying extravaganzas.

The Chinese government is also seeking to confirm its new global status by investing in its space program. Though China did not stage its first manned space flight until 2003, the country has plans to construct a permanent space station and send astronauts to the moon. This comes at a time when the United States and Russia, for decades the major players in space exploration, are scaling down their programs. At the moment, it seems that the Chinese leadership is willing to spend the money necessary to make the PRC the global leader in space within a decade or two.

What is the "One-Child Family" Policy?

This name, often used in the West to refer to China's post-1979 birth control program, is somewhat misleading—hence my use of quotation marks.

It is misleading first because exceptions have always been made that allow some couples to have more than a single child, including, for most of the drive's history, non-Han couples, and second, because it has been less a unified national policy—suggesting an overall plan for implementation—than a multifaceted effort to promote a target for population limitation, which local officials are expected to reach via means of their own devising.

The basic aim of the drive is simple: to limit the size of Chinese families, by ensuring that most couples have one or at most two children. A mixture of methods has been used to achieve this goal, ranging from implementing an intensive publicity campaign to pressuring people with one or two off-spring to have no more.

There were many reasons this policy was bound to draw criticism in the West—and particularly in the United States, given the volatility of American debates about abortion. Some demographers questioned whether, even though China had a baby-boom generation reaching childbearing age in the late 1970s and 1980s (Mao had pronounced that a great strength of the PRC was the vast number of people it had), policies this stringent were ever needed to keep the country's population in check. And recently there have been signs of a loosening of strictures on birth rates, due to worries that the nation will face a labor shortage as its number of senior citizens burgeons.[17]

In addition, international opponents of abortion, a particularly significant group in the United States (a minority but a very vocal one), were angered that family-planning workers treated this as an ordinary method for ending an unwanted pregnancy. The pressure put on local officials to ensure that their communities met stringent birth limitation quotas meant that there were, from the start, inevitably cases in which young women were pressured unduly to terminate their pregnancies, even bullied or forced into having abortions.

Many Americans were prone to view with distaste a setting in which the government interfered so intensely in matters thought of as deeply private concerns, as occurred when work units used "period police" to monitor whether women were menstruating, and when bureaucrats made a family's decision about when exactly to start a family and how many children they could have.[18] There were also disturbing echoes of discredited eugenic ideas in some of the propaganda that accompanied the policy initially, which referred to the need for fewer but "better" children to be born—though this was partly offset when exemptions to have additional offspring were granted to China's fifty-five official recognized *shaoshu minzu* (literally, minority nationalities; i.e., everyone who is not ethnically Han Chinese).

Was female infanticide encouraged to help limit population size?

No—though sometimes Americans have erroneously thought this was the case.

The early 1980s did see a resurgence of female infanticide (a practice that was known in prerevolutionary China but diminished rapidly after 1949) and there were also some sex-selective abortions by couples determined to have at least one son. The combination of these two things led to skewed sex ratios in some rural locales, where many more boys than girls survive the first years of childhood—a phenomenon that many inside the PRC view not only as morally troubling but also as something that could have profound social consequences as young men become frustrated by the lack of potential marriage partners.[19]

Where misunderstanding has come in has been when, in the United States, Chinese female infanticide and sex-selective abortions have been presented as part of the One-Child Policy. Far from being true, these actions, and husbands' (or in-laws') abusing women who bear daughters instead of the sons they would prefer, are better understood as acts of *resistance* to the One-Child Policy. After all, one of its key tenets, as evidenced by the constant use of happy lone infant daughters on posters extolling the virtues of small families, has been that couples should be just as delighted to have a single female child as a single male one.[20]

When family members show displeasure with female children or, in the most extreme cases, end the lives of these infants, they are going against—not conforming to—dictates from on high. The Chinese government can be taken to task for failing to fight hard enough to counter the preference for sons. And some recent policies have inadvertently worked to reinforce the bias toward male children. Most notably, in a time of increasing privatization of agriculture, in a country where it has never stopped being the norm for rural brides to move to their husbands' households (this is one thing that the New Marriage Law of 1950 did nothing to alter), there is a strong economic incentive to have a child who is likely to bring labor power into the family via marriage. A woman, on the other hand, takes her labor with her when she marries and departs, so that her labor power benefits her in-laws more than it does her own parents. There is a difference, however, between saying that the Chinese authorities could have done much more to minimize female infanticide or that their policies inadvertently contributed to its rise and saying that it was an element of government policy.

Is contemporary China utterly unique?

China's current hybrid economic and political system defies easy categorization, and the PRC's post-Mao and (to an even greater extent) post-Tiananmen trajectory seems to have broken several basic rules of historical development. Never before has a process of industrialization and urbanization occurred so rapidly, and on a canvas so vast. This makes China's rise seem very different from the rapid growth that occurred in nearby Asian countries, such as Singapore.

In addition, no other Communist Party has ever overseen a period of runaway economic growth like China's. This sets the CCP apart not just from the state socialist regimes that fell from power late in the last century but also from the enduring ones, such as that of North Korea, with its failing economy, and those of Cuba and Vietnam (each doing much better than North Korea but still not experiencing successive years of high growth rates comparable to those of the PRC).

There is, moreover, something special about the way that China confounds categorization along a capitalist/socialist axis. For example, many countries, including Scandinavian ones such as Sweden, can be aptly described as combining elements of "capitalism" and "socialism," and there are also many nations (including the United States) where the line between the governmental and private sectors can get very blurry, thanks in part to officials in one administration becoming consultants to industry as soon as they are out of power. Still, the borders in today's China between its "capitalist" and "socialist" and "bureaucratic" and "business" sectors are especially tricky to draw.

This is because China's boom has been fueled by entrepreneurial activity and foreign investment, yet large state-run enterprises not only remain in operation but also continue to be a major force within the overall economy. Moreover, many of the new "private" companies one hears about turn out to be run by the children of CCP leaders, and some luxury hotels that seem to epitomize the anti-capitalist Maoist state's retreat are business ventures of the People's Liberation Army that Mao once led to victory.[21]

It is useful up to a point to think of China as a country of "crony capitalism," a term that has been used to describe certain Latin American countries and India at specific points in its history. Even this phrase, though, does not seem to quite "scratch where it itches" (to borrow a Chinese colloquialism), in terms of accurately characterizing what is going on in the country now.[22]

It is also useful, again up to a point, to view China under the control of leaders who, to borrow a term from Andrew J. Nathan, engage in adaptive authoritarianism. This would place it in the category of other countries, such as Vladimir Putin's Russia, that are the focus of William J. Dobson's 2011 study, *The Dictator's Learning Curve*, a book that emphasizes the degree to which current authoritarian figures make use of new media and take a pragmatic and often only vaguely ideological approach to staying in power. One difference here, though, is that while many of the countries Dobson focuses on are run by charismatic individuals, recent

Chinese leaders, especially the colorless Hu Jintao, are any-thing but.

In light of contradictory and confusing factors such as these, and given how difficult it is to place the PRC into any of the categories routinely used to categorize nations, it is easy to see why many analysts have felt that it is best to character-ize China by way of newly coined terms that emphasize its unusual aspects. Nicholas Kristof, for example, has created the neologism "Market-Leninism," and some political sci-entists have referred to "capitalism with Chinese character-istics" (a play upon official talk of "socialism with Chinese characteristics").[23] These terms have value, but it is dangerous to overstate China's exoticness. A precise mix of elements does make the PRC's trajectory *sui generis*, but many things going on there parallel those that have occurred or are occurring in other countries.

What does China have in common with other countries?

Many phenomena can be cited to illustrate the seductiveness, but also the problem, with highlighting China's "distinctive-ness" over its commonalities with other countries. Consider, for example, the way China and India tend to be discussed together. The two countries are usually presented as a study in contrasts because only the latter has a federal system (that gives states great autonomy), and the former does not hold elections (while the latter is routinely described as the world's biggest democratic nation). The developmental paths of the "Dragon" and the "Elephant" are seen as representing two very different roads.

There are many ways, however, in which the experiences of the two most populous countries in Asia, and indeed the world, can be compared to highlight similarities, and thereby shed light on one another. The PRC, like India, took its modern form as a nation-state in the 1940s, and in the 1950s economic five-year plans were the order of the day in each country. By the 1960s, Cold War visions of a clear Communist/Free World binary notwithstanding, Chinese and Indian leaders were each trying to find a place for their country that kept it out of both the shadow of the United States and the shadow of the Soviet Union. Then in the late 1970s, both places sought to discover a developmental path that was unique, and Chinese and Indian political figures alike became fascinated by the Singapore model. Despite the enormous differences in scale between this city-state and China and India, Singapore was a polity that had suffered under imperialism and then, after independence, experienced an economic boom.

Once China and India are thought of as sharing important characteristics, in addition to having many distinctive features, developments in one country can be used to illuminate those in the other. The Chinese interest in using mega-events to show that the PRC is now a "modern" rather than a "backward" country, for example, has an Indian parallel. New Delhi hosted the 2010 Commonwealth Games, an Olympic-like spectacle preceded by an ambitious urban redevelopment drive that, while not as costly and over-the-top as that which preceded the Beijing Games, brought to mind the lead-up to 2008 Olympic Opening Ceremonies. There was a great deal of hand-wringing in the Indian press at the time of China's Olympic success because Indians feared it would be difficult for India to put on as polished a show. But this only underlines the similar ambitions within each country to use dramatic acts to shed the sense of backwardness they have carried from a time when Western empires dominated the world.

There are many other topics where China–India comparisons that stress similarity rather than difference can be useful. Take, for instance, the violence that erupted in Xinjiang in the summer of 2009, which the Indian journalist Pallavi Aiyar, who spent several years as the *Hindu* newspaper's Beijing bureau chief, says is often "served up" by the Western press as "the latest evidence of a stand-off between an oppressive dictatorship, and freedom-loving innocents." While this "framing [of] the 'story'" of an event that left 180 people dead (more of them Han Chinese than Uighurs) "fits in neatly with the West's evangelical prescriptions for political change in China," according to Aiyar, "reading the Xinjiang riots as primarily a showdown between the State and citizens is misleading." A more apt approach is to place it into the same category of interethnic, religiously inflected outbursts of communal violence with which the residents of many parts of India have become all too familiar in recent years.

Here is the clear-eyed, concise synopsis of the events leading up to and following the July 2009 violence that Aiyar offers, which approaches the story in a manner free of Cold War categorizations of the sort she criticizes:

> In Xinjiang, members of the indigenous Uighur minority complain of discrimination and racism from the majority Han ethnicity. The Han, in turn, say the Uighurs are a pampered, ungrateful lot. A relatively small incident…lights a match to the tinderbox of communal tensions. Rioting by Uighurs leads to retaliatory rampages by Han. Han and Uighur neighbours, who have lived for years in peace, suddenly look at each other with suspicion….

Echoes of India's own minority–majority clashes are loud and clear.[24]

Aiyar does not gloss over the role that Beijing's policies, including economic ones that have helped Han living in the region get rich faster than others, have played in exacerbating tensions in Xinjiang. But she insists that, when viewed through eyes accustomed to India, to overlook the communal violence side of the problem is to miss one of its most significant features. And she notes that when violence between Muslim and non-Muslim groups breaks out in India, state backing for the latter is often even more lopsided than state backing for the

Han is in Xinjiang. That many more Uighur than Han "rioters" have been arrested in the ongoing crackdown precipitated by the July 2009 violence is certainly an important fact to bring into the picture, but it just adds a further dimension rather than undermining the value of Aiyar's framing of the tale.

China has always been unique in some specific ways, due to its distinctive history and the sheer size of its population, which is rivaled only by that of India. It has also followed a political path that, in certain regards, is unlike that of any other place. However, to make sense of the country's current situation, we need to balance consideration of what sets it apart from other places with how it is like other nations. And one country that Americans should realize has important things in common with today's China, as we will see in the next chapter, is their own.

5

US–CHINA MISUNDERSTANDINGS

What is the most common thing
Americans get wrong about China?

The preceding chapters have drawn attention to some important sources of US misunderstanding of Chinese realities. Discussion of the "One-Child Family" campaign, for example, drew attention to a tendency, which shows up in regard to other issues as well, for Americans to treat unintended side effects of a Chinese government policy as part of the policy itself, while comments on the Tiananmen Uprising showed how recent historical events are sometimes misconstrued. Americans are also inclined—as a result of pronouncements coming out of and pageants staged in Beijing—to accept as a simple truth the mythic notion of an enduring and relatively unchanged "5,000-year-old" Chinese civilization.

The most deeply rooted and persistent US misconception about China, though, deserves some extended discussion. This is Americans' too-limited appreciation of China's diversity, which leads to a view that China is populated by people who are all pretty much alike, or, at least, who can be neatly divided into one large group and a small number of people who stand apart. We have seen examples of this already, including in the mistaken idea that, in political terms, China now has only "loyalists" and "dissidents," but there are many other realms in which either homogeneity or a neat division into two categories is assumed—when it should not be.

Why is China's diversity overlooked?

The mistaken view of China as a homogeneous land goes back hundreds of years. Between Marco Polo's day and World War II, Western audiences were exposed to books and visual materials that presented China as a land of menacing hordes of faceless and essentially interchangeable people who were all hostile to foreigners. Earlier generations of Europeans and Americans in particular were also periodically influenced by a more positive variant of this motif, brought to cinematic glory via the film *The Good Earth*, in which the country was portrayed as composed of village after village of poor yet hardworking (but largely interchangeable) families.[1]

US notions of Chinese homogeneity gained a new lease on life during the first decades of the Cold War era (1949–1989). This was a time when many World War II images of Japan, as a militaristic land in which everyone conformed to the wishes of the madmen in charge of the country, were simply transposed to China, while the Japanese, now allies of the United States, were envisioned as diverse and peaceful. Thanks to the way the Western press covered the Korean War and then the Cultural Revolution, the word "China" began to conjure in many Western minds a picture of lookalike men and women who all wore blue "Mao suits" and followed CCP dictates without question. This vision of Chinese conformity, rooted in part in efforts by the government to create a country where everyone had much in common but given a decidedly negative spin internationally, showed through in book titles such as *Mao Tse-tung: Emperor of the Blue Ants*.

This vision of Chinese homogeneity has been challenged by recent decades of news coverage that stresses differences within China. This coverage, though, sometimes only takes the useful but insufficient baby step of moving from presenting all Chinese as belonging to one group to presenting them as falling into just two groups (e.g., when intellectuals are described as having to choose between being "dissidents" and "loyalists," when many fall into other categories). Still, the "Empire of the Blue Ants" notion has a long half-life, as was evidenced in 1999 when students took to the streets to express their outrage at NATO bombs hitting the PRC embassy in Belgrade. While some Western commentators called this a new form of "Boxerism," one conservative US magazine likened the protesters to the Borg of the *Star Trek* universe, an entity made up of drones without the capacity for independent thought.[2]

In reality, the participants in the demonstrations took part for varied reasons. They conveyed their anger via unapproved as well as approved means (for example, some called for a boycott of American goods, even though official spokesmen insisted there should be no boycotts), and sometimes followed but at other times resisted government efforts to turn the movement into one that served the party's goals. The regime, far from feeling comfortable with the alleged manipulability of the students, moved quickly to get the youths off the streets and back into the classrooms, lest they begin to raise issues relating to national authorities' failings in addition to the behavior of NATO.[3]

How does ethnicity come into the picture?

One reason that Americans tend to overlook the degree of diversity within China is that ethnicity and race loom so large in US discussions of heterogeneity and homogeneity. And China, it is said, is 90 percent Han.

There are specific ways in which China can accurately be described as somewhat *less* heterogeneous than other large countries. It has neither the dizzying religious diversity of India nor the complex linguistic variation of Indonesia, and it does not have as many inhabitants whose parents, grandparents, or great-grandparents were born in distant lands as the United States does. But there is a world of difference between saying the PRC is *somewhat less diverse* in specific ways than other countries and suggesting that its people are mostly *basically the same*. And even when it comes to ethnicity, there turns out to be much that is misleading about even the assumption of relative homogeneity.

Even if one accepts the 90 percent Han number, which is a problematic one (there is always something vexing about trying to define the exact boundaries of such categories), there are many groups of people within this capacious majority catchall group who speak mutually unintelligible dialects and have radically dissimilar customs.[4] To cite just one illustration, the Hakka, or "guest people," scattered around China are considered Han but have many characteristics that, in another context, might easily lead observers to categorize them as "ethnically" distinct from those they live among. There are many historical cases of what would seem ideal typical outbursts of communal violence or "interethnic" conflicts that pit Hakka (who, among many other things that have set them apart from their neighbors, never embraced any form of foot binding, a practice that was itself far less uniform than outsiders have often suggested) against non-Hakka living nearby. The Taiping Uprising (Hong Xiuquan was a Hakka) began with an interethnic dimension and took on a Han-versus-Manchu element later.[5]

How important are regional divides?

Further complicating the issue is the fact that people from various Chinese regions often view one another through a lens of difference that colors the way, for example, Belgians typically regard the French and vice versa. Residents of Beijing view their counterparts in Shanghai as utterly unlike and inferior to them—and Shanghai residents return the favor. The dismissive and dehumanizing terminology that some Han urbanites use for Han migrants from the countryside, in which the former imply or state that the latter are less than fully human or just like animals, resembles what Americans describe as racist when skin color is involved.[6] Location and point of origin are thus a crucial source of diversity in the PRC today, as is when rather than where one was born.

How important are age divides in China?

Generation gaps are present in every part of the world. But the speed with which China has changed in the past several decades makes the one in the PRC a chasm of unusual size.

China's population is aging: the 2010 census counted PRC citizens age sixty and older as 9 percent of the population, up two percentage points from the 2000 census. While China's youth population is much larger—about 17 percent of Chinese are age fifteen or younger—that group is actually shrinking (in 2000, 23 percent were in the 0 to 14 age range).[7] Still, for a large proportion of Chinese, Mao has always been dead, and the Berlin Wall has always been rubble. Switching from political to social issues, about one-fifth of all Chinese were never alive in a PRC that did not have a large divide separating those who have benefitted most from the reforms and those who have been left behind by them, while those between thirty and sixty-five have a memory of more egalitarian times, and those older than that may see the current disparities between "haves" and "have nots" as a return of sorts to an economic division they knew in their childhood.

In cultural terms, most middle-aged urban parents are people who, until they were in their thirties, never made a private call or rode in a car, for the main phones were still shared neighborhood ones and the main urban vehicles still bikes and buses as recently as the first several times I went to China (between the mid-1980s and mid-1990s). And yet, they have children who have always had mobile phones and think nothing of hailing cabs.

This generation gap influences an enormous number of things, from attitudes toward the pace of modern life (this can seem unsettling to some and bracing to others) to views of China's place in the world. And it affects phenomena that are presented as transcending generation.

Consider, for example, the supposedly timeless Chinese attachment to "Confucian" values, such as social harmony. The oldest residents of the PRC can remember a time when China was governed by a non-Communist regime that venerated Confucius and made much of the need to follow his moral dictates. For Chinese born between the mid- to late 1940s and the early 1960s, by contrast, the current celebration of Confucius and his ideas may seem a bit odd, since they may remember mass campaigns to criticize all vestiges of Confucian thought. But for Chinese born recently, who are unfamiliar with this history (it is ignored or glossed over in schoolbooks, and their parents sometimes prefer not to talk about it), there is nothing remarkable at all about Hu's ideas being tied to Confucius.

Is China still truly an atheist state?

Yet another source of Chinese diversity that is sometimes underestimated concerns religion. China is still officially an atheist country, but many religions are growing rapidly, including evangelical Christianity; estimates of how many Chinese have converted to some form of Protestantism range widely, but at least tens of millions have done so. Various hybrid sects that combine elements of traditional creeds and belief systems (Buddhism mixed with local folk cults, for example) are also increasingly popular. This is adding another level to the diversity of the PRC.

The country has always had a significant number of Muslims, some living in Xinjiang (a northwestern autonomous region), but others residing in disparate parts of the country (including Xi'an, home of the famous Terracotta Warriors). And the diversity among China's Christian population has an added dimension because of a divide between officially sponsored and nonofficial versions of some varieties of Christianity. For example, there have long been and still are Catholic congregations in China that are accepted as legitimate by the CCP (but not by Rome) because the priests in charge of them (and the bishops above these priests in the church hierarchy) do not acknowledge the authority of the pope, but there are also now Chinese Catholics who view the papacy in the traditional way.

There are residents of the Tibetan autonomous region and also of neighboring provinces such as Qinghai and Sichuan who are practicing Tibetan Buddhists. In addition, many Chinese have always believed in or have recently become adherents of still other religions, some old (Daoism) and others new (*qigong* sects, whose followers engage in gentle exercise, breathing practices, and meditation to cultivate the self).

Is China a Big Brother state?

In addition to ideas about China that have roots stretching back much further, some US misconceptions about the PRC can be tied to a tendency to think of all countries run by Communist Party regimes as "Big Brother" states. When the Soviet Union existed, it was thought to be the place where the imaginary world of George Orwell's *1984* had come to life. And since the fall of the U.S.S.R., China has often been cast in that same role. Some commentators argue that North Korea fits the bill most neatly, but the adjective "Orwellian" is still often applied to China.

In specific cases it fits very nicely, but this Cold War vision of China obscures the fact that it can be equally or more useful to look to a competing work of dystopian fiction that was published nearly two decades before Orwell's book appeared in June 1949. This book is *Brave New World*, the classic 1932 novel by Aldous Huxley, who was among Orwell's teachers at Eton.[8] Both *1984* and *Brave New World* often show up together on reading lists, and each is set in a future world where individual freedoms are greatly limited. They do, however, present a contrasting vision of authoritarianism, since Orwell emphasizes the role of fear in keeping people in line, while Huxley pays more attention to how needs and desires are created, manipulated, and satisfied.

The use of *1984* and *Brave New World* as contrasting works goes back at least as far as October 1949—the very year that the PRC was established. In a letter to his former student written in that historic month, Huxley noted that *1984* was a "profoundly important" book but that he thought that the kind of "boot-on-the-face" authoritarian regime it described would soon be a thing of the past. In the future, he suspected, ruling oligarchies would find "less arduous" methods for satisfying their "lust" for power. He went on to explicitly state that he expected these rulers to stay in control via the softer means he had sketched out in *Brave New World*, which stresses the depoliticizing effect of keeping people apart and providing them with distracting forms of activity and entertainment.[9]

Here, again, the case of the Internet provides a useful way into a thorny issue relating to China. In this case, the question is whether Orwell or Huxley provides the better guide to making sense of Chinese political and cultural shifts.

The Chinese government's efforts to control the Internet have often been described as "Orwellian," a term that gained particular resonance in June 2009, when Beijing implemented a new set of measures aimed at limiting the ability of residents of the PRC to surf the web freely just as the sixtieth anniversary of *1984*'s publication was being marked in the West.[10] This approach has value, but there is also much to be said for the following statement of Jeremy Goldkorn, who has written frequently about the "Net Nanny" side of Internet control. As Goldkorn has noted, "Most Chinese net users, who go online primarily for entertainment, don't notice and don't particularly care about censorship, as long as they can chat to their friends, play games, listen to music and watch videos. Their dystopia is more *Brave New World* than *1984*."[11]

In bringing together Orwell's "hard" and Huxley's "soft" visions of authoritarianism in discussions of China, a temporal dimension is worth keeping in mind. The Chinese political system has never been and is not now static, for the strategies that the state turns to are always shifting. The pattern has often been for alternating periods of what Chinese authors refer to as "tightening" and "loosening." This was reflected largely in the Mao years, when periods of intense mobilization via mass campaigns and periods of relative quiescence alternated. With mass campaigns now much less common, the interplay between "tightening" and "loosening" is more subtle. For example, there are periods when brave independent journalists and crusading NGOs are given a bit more freedom, and times, such as during the "tightening" period of late 2008 through 2009 and again in early 2011, when several prominent independent intellectuals were imprisoned.

The PRC went through an "Orwellian moment" between 1989 and 1992, which began with the killing of protesters and then a "2 + 2 = 5"-style denial that a massacre had occurred and the detaining of many alleged "black hands" (a CCP term for troublemakers). The PRC had entered a more Huxleyan stretch by the mid-1990s, for by that point—though it continued to deny that there had been a massacre in 1989—the state was focusing largely on fostering a consumer revolution that it hoped would achieve a kind of mass depoliticization. It was occupied, to use the *Brave New World* term for a powerful soporific drug, with producing "Soma-like" effects.

Though there is an ebbing and flowing of "hard" and "soft" forms of authoritarianism over time, a geographical dimension is also involved. In areas with significantly large and periodically restive non-Han populations, such as Xinjiang and Tibet, the modes of control tend to remain much more *1984*, even when the country as a whole is in a *Brave New World* mode. Conversely, in booming East Coast cities such as Shanghai, with their cultures of distraction epitomized by public spaces dominated by massive video screens and their glittering department stores, Huxley tends to be the better guide. And, so far, the former colonies of Hong Kong and Macao have never, since becoming part of the PRC in the late 1990s, been subjected fully to *1984*-like suppression.

What is the biggest source of Chinese misunderstanding of the United States?

Simply put, the biggest source of Chinese misunderstanding of the United States is a failure to appreciate how differently media systems work in China and in the United States.

At the root of this problem, which has ripple effects that influence many other specific sorts of the misunderstanding, is the belief that the US media system as a whole, including venues that are as different from one another as the *New York Times* is from CNN and both are from Fox News, is strongly and unwaveringly biased against the PRC and simply refuses to give it a fair shake. Three things contribute to the staying power of this notion, which has a firm hold in the minds of even some Chinese who have spent time studying in the United States. Understanding what these factors are and how they work together to create a deeply rooted sense of unfairness tells us something important that all foreigners, not just Americans, need to know about China.

One contributing factor is that the US press, like the British press and those in many other countries, is predisposed, in a way that media in the PRC have not been, to emphasize bad news. It is an axiom of Western journalism in general that stories of tragedy and hardship sell more papers (and attract more viewers, whether of websites or of television screens) than do tales of happiness—or, even worse, tales of simple contentment. The PRC media, however, have long focused to an overwhelming degree on positive developments, at least when discussing China (higher living standards, less hunger, faster trains, etc.). Very recently, tabloids, blogs, and Weibo posts that focus on more downbeat tales of woe have become more common and more popular, but in the official media, good news about domestic issues remains the norm. Hence, even if the Western press treats the PRC like any other country, the perception of many Chinese used to rosier sorts of journalism would be that their country was being treated in an unusually harsh way, not in a routine fashion.

A second contributing factor is that it is not common in contemporary China for publications to showcase contrasting views on a topic. Many Chinese assume (usually correctly) that a commentary that appears in a major Beijing or Shanghai newspaper reflects the opinion of its publishers. By contrast, the *New York Times* may run two opinion pieces on a subject by people who disagree, plus an editorial of its own that stakes out a third position. If any one of the three pieces in question attacks China, however, and a translation of it begins to circulate on the web, many Chinese readers will easily assume that this represents the view of the *Times*.

A third contributing factor is that there are simply some issues on which standard Chinese and standard US assumptions diverge so greatly that a perception of bias is almost guaranteed to be generated or reinforced—no matter how the US media handle a PRC story. One way to illustrate this is via the case of the March 2008 conflict in Tibet, which reveals clearly how entering a story from radically different starting points can lead to two sides talking past rather than to one another.

How do US and Chinese views on Tibet differ?

For many Americans, the starting point for thinking about Tibet has tended to be that the Tibetans are a peace-loving and oppressed people, who have, throughout most of their history, been self-governing, and now have a noble leader in exile, the Dalai Lama. He is thought of as an enlightened man, who is so committed to nonviolence that he won a Nobel Peace Prize.

In America, many view the Dalai Lama as someone who has shown great restraint by agitating only for greater cultural autonomy and religious freedom for Tibetans within the PRC, rather than calling for the establishment of an independent state. The vision of the Tibetan struggle as a defense of religious freedom by a people who are under the thumb of a "foreign power," while influential in many parts of the West (and other places), takes on special force in the United States because of its own specific history and nationalist mythology. The US view casts the Tibetans in a role not unlike that played by the New England colonists who took part in the fight against Britain that looms so large in the American patriotic imagination.

The starting point for many citizens of the PRC who are not ethnic Tibetans, by contrast, is radically different. They assume that Tibet has long been part of China and that the traditions of the region are backward and feudal, as evidenced in part by a tendency to express fanatic loyalty to each new Dalai Lama, a man who is ascribed a role that is part monarch and part pope and is considered a reincarnation of his predecessor. This leads to a sense that Tibetans should be grateful to Beijing for having modernized cities such as Lhasa, raised the status of Tibetan women (through laws based on principles of gender equality), and introduced scientific practices to a superstitious land. Some Han Chinese also think that ethnic Tibetans should be grateful for having received various kinds of special treatment from the state (including being allowed to have more than one child, a privilege also afforded members of the country's fifty-four other non-Han ethnicities).

The gulf between the two starting points just described is so vast that those on opposite sides of it are predisposed to view the accounts of any event involving Tibet that are coming from those on the other side of the chasm as completely off base. To place two US analogies side by side, while many in the United States find it natural to place Tibetans who take to the streets into the same general category as the heroic colonists of 1776, many non-Tibetans in the PRC view these same actors more like an average citizen of the United States would view participants in a rowdy rally calling for Hawaii to be returned, in its currently modernized state, to the descendants of the last king of those islands.[12] In such a context, every account of a conflict pitting Tibetan and non-Tibetan residents of Tibet and nearby regions against one another, right down to the choice of words used to describe clashes and individuals, is bound to be contentious. What many Westerners would normally dub a "demonstration," for example, many non-Tibetans in the PRC call a "riot," and in regard to the exiled Tibetan leader whom many Westerners find it natural to see referred to as a "spiritual leader" and "Nobel laureate," many non-Tibetans in the PRC find it natural to see referred to in a derogatory way as a "wolf in monk's clothing," a "separatist," and so on.

The quagmire just described is such that even careful and nuanced foreign reporting on Tibet can end up being interpreted by some Chinese as biased. For example, the most thoughtful US journalists did sometimes use terms such as "riot" to refer to the outbursts of violence in March 2008, and this was fitting, given that there were times when ethnic Tibetan youths attacked local Han Chinese and members of the Hui *minzu* (a Muslim group). But this was still seen by some non-Tibetan readers in the PRC as "biased" reporting, since the authors in question stopped short of blaming the Dalai Lama for the violence (as the official Chinese media did). Less careful reporting, meanwhile, engendered a much stronger sense of unfairness within China. When CNN showed an image of police in Nepal engaging in violence and misidentified the shot as one of Chinese police beating up Tibetans, bloggers throughout the PRC wrote furious post after furious post attacking the Atlanta-based network (an "anti-CNN" website was launched and "Don't Be Like CNN" t-shirts sold in Shanghai), since what might have been simple carelessness was immediately treated by many as just the latest indication of a deep-seated prejudice.

6

THE FUTURE

Is China bent on world domination?

Fears of a military "China threat," which were renewed in some quarters by the massive display of weapons during the 2009 National Day parade, have a long history. They also have a long history of being overblown.

The Boxers never ventured outside of North China or showed any interest in doing so, for example, but this did not stop Kaiser Wilhelm from treating them as the vanguard of a "Yellow Peril" that would spread into the West. And though Mark Twain insisted that the Boxers were just trying to protect their own villages from foreign encroachment in a manner Americans should respect (he called the insurgents China's "traduced patriots" and said he would have become a Boxer himself if he had been born Chinese), some of his compatriots embraced the apocalyptic view of the German leader. One US magazine described the Boxers as constituting the greatest Asian threat to the West and Christendom since Genghis Khan's Mongol forces had swept into Europe in the 13th century.

The notion of a Yellow Peril threatening the West later gave way to that of a Red Menace emanating from Beijing. This idea gained purchase in the early 1960s, when Beijing produced its first atom bomb. Coming at a time when anti-imperialist rhetoric ran high in the PRC, this was a frightening development to the two countries, the United States and the Soviet Union, that Mao was denouncing most vociferously—the former for its capitalism and support of Taiwan, and the latter for its "revisionist" abandonment of Marxism.

The US war office even produced a film, "Red Chinese Battle Plan," in the 1960s that presented Beijing as intent upon global control. Updating imagery used in 1940s propaganda films that had showed China as one of the innocent victims of Japanese plans for world domination, the PRC was presented as seeking to first gain control of Africa and Latin America and then moving to take over the United States. Getting the bomb was unquestionably important to China, but we now know that the PRC was so beset by internal problems and border disputes with neighboring countries such as Russia and India that there was no real likelihood of its military threatening any distant land. China did seek allies in the nonaligned states of the developing world, presenting itself as an ideologically attractive alternative to the United States and the U.S.S.R. Still, fears of a Chinese Red Menace reaching into North America were just as much the product of overheated imaginations as the Yellow Peril fantasies of an earlier era. The Red Menace fears were no more rooted in reality than were the Yellow Peril ones expressed, for example, by a political cartoon from 1900 that showed a bloodthirsty Boxer wrapping his knife-wielding arms around the globe, and in the following decades by Sax Rhomer novels about the diabolically cunning and remorselessly violent Western-hating arch-villain Fu Manchu.

Proxy wars between the US and Communist countries did occur between the 1950s and 1970s. And there were times when cross-strait skirmishes between the Communists of Beijing and the Nationalists of Taipei, each of whom claimed to be the sole rightful rulers of all of China, could have escalated into a direct war between the PRC and the United States. But there was no serious Chinese plan for world domination then. And there is none now.

China has been spending increasing amounts of money on its military, which has been modernized into an impressive fighting force. This is and should be a source of concern to its immediate neighbors and countries with which it has ongoing border disputes. But the build-up of the PLA is not just about having the ability to project force abroad. For example, the Chinese regime still thinks of itself as needing to ensure that China is not attacked (the NATO bombing raids against Serbia and the coalition invasions of Iraq and Afghanistan have helped keep this sense of the need for a strong defense alive). And, at least as significantly, it also sees having a powerful military as crucial for maintaining control at home. It was the PLA, not a civilian police force, that carried out the June 4th Massacre, after all, and the government relies on the army to deal with unrest in places such as Tibet and Xinjiang. The showcasing of military hardware during National Day parades can, in fact, be seen as being as much an effort to remind domestic audiences of the sophistication of the weaponry of the state as an effort to make an impact on foreign observers.

How likely is a war with Taiwan?

There are many factors that make it extremely unlikely that the PRC will use military force to try to achieve the long-held goal of "reunification," which remains a stated desire of both the CCP and the Nationalist Party but is not even an aim of the organizations with which the latter now has to share power in Taiwan. The CCP still clings to the idea that there is only "one China" (a notion that the political separation of Taiwan from the Mainland is a temporary aberration rather than a permanent state of affairs), but it is hard to see how it would end up acting to change reunification from a far-off dream to an immediate reality. The possibility of war cannot be discounted completely. There is always the chance that, if the CCP felt that it were in danger of falling, it might make a desperate bid at shoring up popular support by taking a dramatic and perhaps even foolish course of action, such as a raid against Taiwan, that it hoped would appeal to extreme nationalist sentiment. Still, there are two main things that are working at present to minimize the likelihood of this happening.

First, money and people are moving across the straits regularly and in ways that benefit both countries. There are by some estimates as many as half a million citizens of the ROC who live and work in Shanghai; there are many Taiwanese businesses with offices on the Mainland; and there are now, for the first time in decades, starting to be direct flights between Taipei and cities in the PRC, particularly at holiday times, when travelers want to cross the straits to visit family members.

Second, the current relationship between Beijing and Hong Kong provides a means of imagining a future in which the Taiwan issue is resolved. Hong Kong residents were promised that they would retain a great deal of autonomy for fifty years after 1997, under a policy called "One Country, Two Systems," which would allow different laws to govern local activities in the former Crown colony until 2047, while it became integrated into the PRC in other regards.

There was a great deal of skepticism about what this would mean in practice, and there have been criticisms since 1997 about Beijing's efforts to rein in various aspects of Hong Kong political, economic, and cultural life, and about the press becoming less free due to a mixture of outside pressure and self-censorship. Without dismissing these concerns (there is a basis to them, and the fact that Hong Kong has remained as independent of Beijing as it has so far is due partly to bold forms of resistance by activists and local residents), the degree to which the city has been able to retain a degree of autonomy remains striking. Bookstores in Hong Kong still carry many publications—from works by the Dalai Lama to Chang and Halliday's biography of Mao, from collections of manifestos issued during the Tiananmen protests to a memoir by Zhao

Ziyang written secretly while he was under house arrest—that are banned on the Mainland. Falun Gong adherents, though hassled, can still publicize their cause in Hong Kong. And, in general, partly because of China's desire to keep business thriving, Hong Kong is able to function as both a region of the PRC and as something a bit like a city-state.

This makes it possible to imagine a time when some similar sort of arrangement is worked out that would allow Taiwan, which by then would already be thoroughly enmeshed with the Mainland economically and culturally, to be formally brought into the orbit of the PRC without giving up its identity. This is not something that citizens of Taiwan necessarily want to see happen, and there is still a wait-and-see attitude toward Hong Kong in that city and among foreign observers. Just the fact that a "One Country, Three Systems" future can be contemplated, even as a far-fetched scenario, though, minimizes the likelihood of war.

Will China become the world's dominant economic power?

There are good reasons to think that the United States will still be the world's dominant economic power for some time to come. It is a sign of just how much the PRC and its place in the world have changed in recent times, though, that questions such as this even seem sensible to ask. Fifty years ago—indeed, even twenty years ago—when people speculated about China's future, this just was not something they pondered.

In the late 1950s, Mao had boasted that the utopian Great Leap Forward would allow the country to catch up with the West quickly in metrics of development such as amounts of steel produced. Very few people outside of the country, though, took these assertions seriously when he made them.

By the early 1960s, with the Great Leap clearly a failure, it would have seemed nothing short of ridiculous to consider that, in a mere half century, the PRC could move to the top ranks of economic powers. Had outsiders known, as few if any did, the full extent of the horrific famine under way, they would have been even more dismissive of China's prospects of rising to the top tier of economic powers within the next fifty years. The best that was expected was that it would go from a fairly poor developing country to an only somewhat impoverished one. In contrast to today, when the PRC sometimes exports food to famine-struck countries, the economic question of the day was whether China would be able to feed its own population.

Yet, against all odds, China's current economic rank is second; only the United States stands higher in terms of gross domestic product. The long series of years of high—even double-digit—growth rates that it experienced just before and after the turn of the millennium changed it from a poor country to one that, while not rich (per capita income is still far behind that of developed countries), has enough wealth to help other countries when they are hit by disasters. It is now easy to conceive of a point coming, before another fifty years have passed, when it will have caught up with the United States in some reckonings of economic strength and surpassed it in others, though it is still unlikely that it will surge far ahead of the United States as an economic power in the foreseeable future when measured in GDP, even if it does edge past it. It is more unlikely still that China will by that point have a population as well off in terms of per capita income, as by that metric the PRC is still a fairly poor country, just not nearly as poor as it was two or three decades ago.

Will China, long thought of as a land of villages, soon be a land of cities?

The question of China's world economic domination revolves in part around the pace of the PRC's transformation from a rural to an urban society, from a land of villages to a land of factories. China circa 1960 was a country that seemed very likely to remain largely rural forever. This is because the CCP had developed rigid and complex social-welfare and social-control mechanisms to check the rural-to-urban movement of people. Such movement had been common between the late 1800s and 1940s, when the population of cities such as Shanghai swelled into the millions, and it is happening again. Somewhere between 150 million and 200 million internal migrants have headed into Chinese cities seeking work. This is more than moved across the Atlantic to the United States when it was industrializing, making China the site of the largest voluntary migration in the history of the world, as Leslie T. Chang has noted.[1]

The main thing inhibiting villagers from relocating to cities during the Mao years was the *hukou,* or "household registration" system, which tied state-provided benefits to remaining in the locale in which one was born. Only in rare instances did individuals receive permission to move, except for betrothed women, who often switched households when they married. Though the CCP worked to alter other features of gender relations, they allowed this pattern of brides moving to continue. Nevertheless, the result was that those born into farming families had no choice but to work the land throughout their lives and have children who remained in villages.

Thanks to the reforms implemented by Deng Xiaoping and his erstwhile protégé Zhao Ziyang, the *hukou* system had become less rigid by 1990. Though the reforms did not entirely dismantle the system, it began to be easier for villagers to go to cities to find seasonal work and sometimes stay there long term.

Thanks to a recent uptick in rural-to-urban migration, and the partial though still not full dismantling of the *hukou* system, China is becoming a country of cities. In early 2012, the Chinese government announced that the country's urban population exceeded its rural one for the first time in history. The 1990 census reported that China already had dozens of urban centers with more than 1 million residents. Today, there are at least 160 cities with populations of a million or more, and about a dozen of those are megacities with 10 million-plus residents. Some of these cities, such as Shenzhen—a southern metropolis that was among the first "special economic zones," in which joint-venture enterprises that brought Chinese and foreign investors together are governed by looser rules than state-run companies—had been mere clusters of villages and towns just a decade or so earlier.

Is China likely to become a democracy?

In the years immediately following the June 4th Massacre, some Western observers wondered if a sequel to the Tiananmen protests or a Chinese counterpart to the Polish Solidarity struggle would lead to China's democratization. More recently, those hoping for a dramatic shift in how the PRC is governed have put their faith in other forces. Some have bet on the Internet doing the trick: both conservative pundit George Will and former president Bill Clinton, who disagree about so many things, went on record around the turn of the millennium with predictions that, once new media took hold in China, a new form of politics would inevitably follow. Others have put their faith in a rising middle class, citing South Korea and Taiwan as examples of authoritarian states that were democratized under pressure from professionals and entrepreneurs.

Any of these things could happen at some point, but none of the predictions have so far been borne out. One reason for this is that the CCP has been working tirelessly to learn how to avoid precisely the scenarios alluded to above. Ironically, for this reason, the constant predictions of the party's imminent demise may have made its fall less rather than more likely.

But while many observers acknowledge that democracy is a remote possibility for China, others express hope for at least some political reforms in the coming years. This conversation was especially intense leading up to the 18th Party Congress in November 2012, when Hu Jintao left office as general secretary of the CCP (and chairman of the Central Military Commission) and Xi Jinping took the reins as China's new leader, expected to serve two five-year terms. Very little is known about Xi, who comes from a "princeling" family and, after a stint in the countryside during the Cultural Revolution, worked his way up the party hierarchy largely by playing it safe. He does, however, have a reputation as an economic reformer, and based on this, some assert that Xi and his second-in-command, Li Keqiang, will pursue moderate political reforms. Others say this is less likely, given that the remaining five members of the Politburo Standing Committee (which, for all intents and purposes, runs the country) are known as being more conservative. Whatever reforms may come, though, are almost surely a few years off, as Xi is likely to spend the initial period of his administration consolidating power and building up a network of supporters.[2]

How will the Hu Jintao era be remembered?

Those watching the 2012 leadership transition with memories of the 2002 transition in mind likely found the speculation about Xi Jinping's reformist inclinations familiar. That is because similar rhetoric surrounded Hu Jintao and Wen Jiabao when they took over leadership of the country in 2002. Those high hopes for reform, however, were dashed during the dreary Hu–Wen administration, which turned out to be characterized largely by compromise in the name of consensus, and was shaped by a desire for political stability that trumped any bold vision the pair might have had. After the heady days of the Beijing Olympics passed, stagnation set in: China's previously stratospheric economic growth slowed amid the 2008 global economic crisis (though the country's economy fared much better than that of many others), and popular discontent with the leadership's lack of clear direction seems to have grown. In what is becoming a familiar refrain—the same could be said about both Mao and Deng—Hu's main problem seems to have been that he remained in power too long. Had he left office immediately after the Olympics, or even after his first term as party secretary ended in 2007, he would likely have a much more positive legacy than the one he carries now.

How powerful is Chinese nationalism?

In the West, a false notion is currently circulating that Chinese nationalism has become something that can only bolster the regime. The assumption is that patriotic fervor serves to prop up the official status quo and that popular nationalism is a force that the authorities can turn on and off like a tap.

The current generation of Chinese has indeed been reared on a steady diet of patriotic propaganda that emphasizes the humiliations that China suffered at the hands of foreign powers during such events as the Opium War (1839–1842) and the Japanese invasions of the 1930s and 1940s. Its members have been encouraged by the state to be wary of contemporary Western bias against the PRC, which is allegedly evidenced by such things as unfair presentations of unrest in Xinjiang and Tibet. And sometimes they comply, as when they briefly called for a boycott of French goods after President Sarkozy of France met with the Dalai Lama in 2008. Likewise, they have been encouraged to fill cyberspace with tirades against any Japanese politician who visits the controversial Yasukuni Shrine—a site that honors the souls of all of Japan's war dead, which includes a vast number of ordinary soldiers, but also several Class A war criminals responsible for brutal policies toward the populations of China and other Asian countries.

Nonetheless, it is still overly simplistic to think that the payoff for a patriotic education is a mass of angry youths ready to do the PRC's bidding whenever it feels like calling on them. In reality, nationalism remains a double-edged sword, which does at times buttress the regime but can also develop in ways that threaten the political status quo.[3] While it is true that patriotic propaganda has shaped the views of young Chinese, there are complex variations in the way they express their love of country and the degree to which this dovetails with official nationalism. China's leaders are well aware that some of the biggest challenges faced by previous Chinese regimes, up to and very much including the Tiananmen Uprising, have been driven in part by patriotic fervor.

They also know that a protest that begins as a loyalist expression of nationalism can evolve into a struggle in which questions are raised about their leadership. And they know that oppositional themes can slip in at times even during demonstrations that are in part officially stage-managed affairs. This was the case in September 2012, when slogans referring to anger over corruption and a wish for China's current leaders to be more like Mao made appearances in state-sanctioned anti-Japanese protests associated with a string of tiny islands over which both Beijing and Tokyo claim sovereignty. The authorities know that once mobilized, patriotic fervor always has the potential to work against rather than for them, and this explains why they often find themselves working to douse as opposed to fan the flames of youthful nationalist ardor.[4] Thus, Chinese nationalism is a Janus-faced force that can and does move easily in both loyalist and oppositional directions.

What kind of government will China have in a decade?

Soon after the turn of the millennium, much of the debate about China was framed in terms of the allegedly contrasting visions spelled out in two books: *China's Democratic Future* (which predicted a smooth transition away from authoritarianism) and *The Coming Collapse of China* (which predicted the country's implosion). Now, however, many experts see the main contrast as that which separates the expectation of dramatic political change (something both books confidently predicted was in the offing) from the possibility of continuity.

The most sophisticated analysts who see continuity as more likely stress that this does not mean a complete lack of change.

They argue for the need to think of the CCP as a protean organization, which has proved capable of adapting itself to the needs of particular moments. They refer to "adaptive authoritarianism" as the best way to categorize PRC politics.

Some of these scholars note, moreover, that there are long roots to this adaptive authoritarianism, which go back much further than the start of the Reform era.[5] Mao was modifying standard Marxist theory and Leninist visions of the party's role as far back as his 1927 "Report on the Hunan Peasant Movement," with its call for Communist organizers to learn from the tactics that villagers were using on the ground, rather than seeing themselves as arriving on the scene as teachers of an innately reactionary rural population.

Then, in the 1930s and 1940s, while an opposition organization, the Communist Party tried many things, including its pioneering use of guerrilla warfare strategies, which departed dramatically from traditional practice. And there were departures from orthodoxy again during the era of high Maoism (the late 1950s through the mid-1970s). For example, many people insisted at that time that a "bad" class status could be passed on from one generation to the next via bloodlines (something that defies the central tenet of Marxism that links class to one's relationship to the means of production).

The fact is that the party, for better or for worse, has shown itself ready to experiment throughout its history, both before and after it seized national power. We should thus not be surprised by its proclivity to keep experimenting today, as it maneuvers to stay in power. It is, by nature, an adaptive organization, and this is important to keep in mind, even if many of the specific experiments that the regime has tried recently, such as treating Confucius as a hero worthy of veneration and claiming that "socialism with Chinese characteristics" can be achieved by expanding rather than limiting the importance of private property, are ones of which Mao, the first great CCP innovator, would have thoroughly disapproved—so thoroughly that I would be tempted to describe these innovations as having set Mao turning over in his grave.

What big challenges lie ahead for the CCP?

If I were a member of the Beijing leadership, five issues would keep me up at night. These might be called (since the CCP likes slogans with numbers) the Three E's and the Two C's: economy, environment, and energy, and corruption and credibility.

All political leaders have to worry about the economy, since people in democracies often vote their pocketbooks, and in authoritarian settings material issues often decide whether people will take to the streets or stay at home. There is, however, a special dimension to the issue in the PRC today. The party has come to depend so heavily on high growth rates that it needs the economy to perform not just well, but *very* well.

This is because, while the economic boom has produced winners and losers, the losers have been able to content themselves with the idea that their turn will come. An end to high growth rates would be deeply unsettling. While frustrating the rising expectations of those who have been doing well, it would also engender a sense of outrage and desperation among those who have been thinking that they will get a chance at some point to experience good times.

Hu Jintao and company tried to do some advance damage control, mainly by working to shore up social services in the countryside, where many of those who have been missing out so far on the benefits of the economic boom have been feeling the negative effects of a shift away from state support for basic things such as health care and education. Xi and company will likely continue these efforts. This certainly has the potential to help, but it is likely to do so only if there continues to be a sense that the economy as a whole is moving in a positive direction. The regime has become both psychologically and practically dependent on high growth rates contributing to a general sense of optimism, which leads to a belief that, whatever its failings may be, the party remains legitimate because it is overseeing a period of impressive economic development and an overall rise in living standards.

What big issues relating to the environment and energy does China face?

Environmental and energy concerns are important to all governments, and, as with the economy, they raise a particular set of dilemmas for China's leaders. And the two topics are tightly intertwined—so much so that it makes sense to consider them together.

The good news for China, as it continues to industrialize, is that it has a good supply of two sources of power: coal deposits (thanks to trucks and railroads, the CCP is not disadvantaged the way the Qing were by these being located far from major cities) and water (which can be used to generate electricity via dams). The bad news is that coal mining and hydraulic projects have their dangerous sides. With coal, the dangers include staggeringly high injury and death rates for miners; though the death rate has steadily fallen over the past decade, there were still almost 2,000 mining-related fatalities in 2011.[6] When coal is used for heating, it creates filthy air—a health issue and potentially also a political one, given the increasing tendency for concerns about pollution to generate protests. The bad news with hydraulic energy is that massive dams have been controversial, leading to protests by locals directly affected by the projects, which almost inevitably require villages to be flooded, and worries about the risks of construction errors.

The bigger bad news for China on the energy front is that demand for oil is rising rapidly, as the country becomes one with more and more drivers, and it keeps needing more and more electricity as well to keep factories humming and provide lights and air conditioning to more and more people living middle-class lifestyles in the country's booming cities.

China has oil reserves (some in politically sensitive areas, like Xinjiang, and near Pacific islands that are claimed by both the PRC and either Vietnam or Japan), but not enough to meet its growing needs. This increases Beijing's determination to have access to foreign suppliers. As with the United States, this shapes international behavior: it is one reason the CCP is so intent on extending its influence in Africa and South America and staying on good terms with Iran.

In terms of electricity, dams and nuclear plants partly help meet demand in the short run, but the country already relies very heavily on coal-burning plants, which generate three-quarters of its electricity. And over the longer term, if this pattern continues, even more of these greenhouse-gas-emitting plants (on average, a new one opens each week) will be needed to keep up the country's breakneck pace of development.

Perhaps the biggest resource-related concern, though, is water. Due to polluted rivers, melting Himalayan ice caps, and a declining North China water table (which was never in good shape to begin with: per capita water amounts there have long been well below 10 percent of the global average), shortages of drinking water and water for irrigation are already a serious problem and are likely to get much worse in the years to come. Water also poses many potential political problems, since some Chinese damming projects stop rivers that run through the PRC from feeding into ones that flow through neighboring countries at their usual rate.[7]

Why are corruption and credibility concerns for the CCP?

In his final work report as CCP party secretary, delivered at the 18th Party Congress in November 2012, Hu Jintao warned that corruption could prove the party's greatest challenge and undermine the legacy of its achievements.[8] Hu had good reason to issue this warning, since 2012 was a trying year for the CCP where corruption was concerned. In February, the police chief of the massive municipality of Chongqing, in the country's southwest, fled to the US consulate in nearby Chengdu. There, he apparently revealed that Chongqing's party secretary, the charismatic politician Bo Xilai, was involved in an elaborate murder and cover-up. Over the following months, a story of sorts (though many details remain murky) came out. Bo's wife, Gu Kailai, had been involved in illegal business dealings, including money laundering, and may have also carried on an extramarital affair with the English businessman who was her partner in many of those deals, Neil Heywood. Gu allegedly felt threatened by Heywood and, with one of her household employees, poisoned him and then covered up his murder. While no one (so far) has claimed that Bo himself was involved in murdering Heywood, this proved the opportunity that his political opponents needed to take down the formerly rising star (some had previously thought that Bo might have a chance to make it onto the nine-member Politburo Standing Committee when the Party Congress was held in November). Bo was dismissed from his position as Chongqing party secretary, stripped of party membership, and will possibly face the death penalty for his crimes, which include decades of graft and extortion.

Bo was not the only high-ranking party official under fire during 2012. Both incoming president Xi Jinping and outgoing premier Wen Jiabao found their families the targets of exposés by foreign news organizations, Bloomberg News and the *New York Times*, respectively.[9] While neither Xi nor Wen is personally accused of misdeeds, Bloomberg and the *Times* documented in impressive detail the ways that their extended families had grown rich through their connections with the politicians and the influence that lent them. None of this is particularly surprising—the reaction of most Chinese seems to have been that the exposés merely confirmed what was already widely assumed—but the reports were nonetheless damaging to the credibility of the CCP, a party that has its origins in promises to reduce inequality in society. In retaliation, the government blocked the Bloomberg and *New York Times* websites.

These are especially high-profile cases of corruption within Chinese politics, and they might not seem to affect the day-to-day lives of ordinary people. What should be of far greater concern to the leadership are the many scandals involving food safety, shoddy construction, and environmental degradation, which are felt at every level of society and stir up anger that cuts across geographic and class boundaries. Environment-related protests, in particular, have been on the rise in recent years, and journalist Christina Larson argues that addressing environmental issues should be the new leadership's top priority if it wants to maintain social stability.[10]

One reason to fear accidents involving shoddy dam construction, which could lead to disastrous flooding, is that corrupt deals are so often cut between officials and builders, who are either related to one another by blood or linked via *guanxi* (literally, "connections," but in China also implying a strong sense of mutual indebtedness established by friendship, bribery, past favors, having been classmates, or some combination of all of these things). In China, the biggest source of anger after the earthquake of 2008 was that so many schools collapsed, killing children. Bloggers asserted from the moment this happened that this was due to developers with ties to local officials cutting corners and only pretending to take costly measures to ensure the soundness of the structures. It is telling that these claims were immediately believed by a great many people; the fact that some roughly comparable buildings near schools were left standing added to the plausibility of the criticism, but the main reason that it was accepted initially was just that it is taken for granted that this kind of thing happens all the time.

The cumulative effect of scandals like those discussed here is that the Chinese government seems to have little credibility among the people it rules. When drenching rains hit Beijing in July 2012 and flooded the city, few believed the official death reports, almost automatically assuming that the death toll resulting from the floods was much higher. Like the boy who cried wolf, the CCP has lied too many times for the public to trust anything it says.

To date, however, disgust with official corruption has not been strong enough to galvanize a new nationwide set of protests that might result in a repeat of the Tiananmen protests of 1989. One reason is that the general economic trend has been upward, which is important because it suggests that, as bad as corruption is, it is not hindering development. The other reason is that the central government has succeeded, for now, in convincing people to go along with the notion that it is local officials who should bear the brunt of criticism. Circling back to the first of the Three E's, one effect of a major economic downturn or even an extended slowdown would be to undermine the sense that corruption is not a roadblock to the achievement of a level of relatively widespread prosperity. The Achilles heel for the CCP, which first rose to power in part because people felt its cadres were less corrupt than Nationalist officials, continues to be the sense that it is as riddled with corruption as the organization it defeated in 1949 once was.

How can the United States and China adjust to an era in which they are the two superpowers?

The issue of the United States and China sharing the stage as the world's two superpowers is a pressing one, and it would be nice to be able to end this book with some simple guidelines for getting beyond or at least lessening the kinds of mutual misunderstandings described in the previous chapter, as there are bound to be tensions enough between China and the United States over tangible issues, without a failure to see one another clearly exacerbating the situation. There are, alas, no easy solutions. As already hinted at above, however, there is at least one thing that might, in a small way, help to combat both US misunderstanding of the PRC and Chinese misunderstanding of the United States. This would be a broader appreciation in both countries of the fact that they have much in common.[11]

More attention could be paid to the fact that some things happening in China today are much like things that happened in the United States when it was industrializing rapidly and rising in global prominence in the late 1800s and early 1900s. And more could be done to underline the fact that, even though leaders often present the two countries as completely unlike one another, people in other parts of the world sometimes view the PRC and the United States as belonging in the same category.

One of the first times I became aware of how similar the United States and China can appear to people living in neither country was when I was invited to Sweden in the 1990s to give a talk on human rights debates between Beijing and Washington. One theme in that lecture was to be the contrast between the enormous emphasis that documents produced in the United States put on the references to civil and religious liberties and free speech issues found in United Nations proclamations, on the one hand, and the enormous emphasis that documents produced in the PRC put on the references to social and economic rights in those same texts. This made it possible, I planned to note, for US officials to present the PRC as an outlier country when it came to human rights offenses (due to Beijing's record of imprisoning dissidents), at the same time that Chinese officials presented the United States as an outlier country when it came to human rights offenses (due to Washington's failure to do away with problems such as homelessness and people lacking health coverage, despite the United States being a rich country).

When I went to a campus radio station for an interview prior to my talk, however, the student host quickly made it clear that, to her (and perhaps to many Swedes), the United States and the PRC were both outlier states when it came to human rights. This is because she began by focusing on the death penalty, stating that for her, this was a major human rights issue, and that the United States and the PRC stood out as two prominent countries that, unlike most great powers, still executed prisoners.

International relations are another area where, despite a desire by Washington and Beijing to emphasize contrasts, some people in other parts of the world are struck by similarities between the United States and China. There are intellectuals based in Europe and India, for example, who note that Washington and Beijing both seem to share a penchant for going to great lengths to protect access to oil—a point that some American critics of US foreign policy sometimes note as well.

Furthermore, this line of argument continues, the leaders of each country have a longstanding tendency of insisting that their country is rooted in an abhorrence of "imperialism" in all its forms, and yet each country has been perfectly ready at times to impose its own visions of "modernity" and "civilization" upon unwilling populations.[12] The implication is that, when thinking about Beijing's policies toward Tibet and Xinjiang, it is useful for Americans to be mindful of how dismissive many in the United States would be of the idea that Hawaii is not really part of the country (it became a state in the same year, 1959, that the Dalai Lama went into exile); how eager Washington has seemed at times to transform Iraq (like Xinjiang, Iraq is a region whose oil reserves the United States wants to be able to tap in the future) into a country that is "autonomous" yet firmly within the US sphere of influence; or, perhaps more strikingly, how China is now handling the population of its frontier zones is seemingly very reminiscent of how the United States treated Native American populations in the 19th century. None of these analogies are perfect, but each of them has enough going for it that it should give pause to those in either country committed to the idea that the

United States and China are lands with completely contrasting traditions.

What other kinds of things do China and the United States have in common?

There are many other parallels, some of which concern precisely the things that Americans are fond of criticizing about the PRC. For example, as Peter Hessler has noted in an article about the "instant cities" of China, where many factories use machines that are pirated versions of US ones, the United States' industrial takeoff was fueled in part by just this sort of "reverse engineering" that allowed businessmen in early US boomtowns to make use, for free, of patented British technologies.[13] And as the US historian Stephen Mihm has pointed out, in the late 1800s, it was the United States that was often seen by Europeans, as China is now often seen by Americans, as a place that produced inferior and sometimes downright dangerous goods and issued pirated editions of best-sellers (Dickens complained bitterly about how many unauthorized versions of his books were sold across the Atlantic).[14] Something else the countries have in common is that between the late 1800s and mid-1900s, the United States built railways and highway systems on a grand scale, which connected parts of the country that were previously cut off from one another and were sometimes hailed as engineering marvels, just as China has been doing (the high-tech train to Tibet being a notable recent case in point). The United States went in for giant dams, just as the Chinese government is doing now. As a recent *Scientific American* article put it: the China of today "is a developing country undergoing an energy transformation unprecedented in human history, but fired by an engineering optimism reminiscent of the U.S. in the 1950s."[15]

That was also the era when the United States hosted its first World's Fairs and first Olympics. And as Susan Brownell, one of the world's leading anthropologists of sports, reminds us, when the United States first got to hold the Games in 1904 (previously, the event had only been held in Europe), some foreign commentators assumed, as they did again during the lead-up to 2008, that the IOC had made a terrible mistake in letting the Olympics be hosted by a country that might have a booming economy but was clearly not ready for prime time.[16]

Is this an argument for Americans to refrain from all criticism of China?

An increased awareness of similarities such as those just noted need not prevent or even discourage Americans from criticizing things that occur in China, and vice versa. But it does suggest that, as Mihm puts it, "if we want to understand how to deal with China, we could do worse than look to our own history as a guide," and that when Americans take the PRC to task for certain things, a "bit of empathy might even be in order."[17] If the residents of each superpower thought as much about what they have in common as what makes them different, it could even help increase the odds that, whichever way the criticisms fly across the Pacific, they will be delivered in a less arrogant and patronizing fashion than has sometimes been the case in the past.

Another thing that could help ease US–China misunderstandings would simply be for people in each country to know more about the people living in the other. I hope that US readers who have made it to the end of this book feel that they now know a few more basic things about the people of the PRC than they did when they read its first pages. And I look forward to the day when I can point my Chinese friends toward a comparable work that tries to tell them, in a similar spirit of seeking to normalize the experiences of a large and exotic-seeming anti-imperialist empire that stands by the Pacific, "everything they need to know" about the United States.

NOTES

Author's Note

1. Timothy Garton Ash, "Lack of News about China Has Nothing to Do with Bias," *Los Angeles Times*, April 16, 2009.
2. With a few exceptions, such as Chiang Kai-shek and Sun Yat-sen, who remain much better known by other forms of transliteration, Chinese terms and names will be romanized according to the pinyin system used in the People's Republic of China. In instances where this may create confusion, an alternative romanization will be placed in parentheses, as above with Chairman Mao.
3. Robert A. Kapp "Coming Distractions: Two Kinds of Time," *China Beat*, November 12, 2008, http://www.thechinabeat.org/?p=276 (accessed July 18, 2012). I agree that a "new Golden Age" of writing (more accessible for being written in English) on China has arrived, and I would credit the following people as having contributed to it: Evan Osnos, Peter Hessler, Ian Johnson, Lijia Zhang, Howard French, Pankaj Mishra, Leslie T. Chang, Michael Meyer, Rob Gifford, Barbara Demick, Tania Branigan, Christina Larson, Mara Hvistendahl, Adam Minter, Gady Epstein, James Miles, Alec Ash, and Pallavi Aiyar. This is a very partial list, and it is limited to those whose main form of communication is the written word (thus it leaves out people who work primarily in radio, such as Louisa Lim); those who began to make their mark in the field of writing about China in the 1990s or later (thus it leaves out people like Isabel Hilton and Orville Schell, who began to do excellent work earlier and continue to write important articles about the PRC); and those who write mainly or exclusively in English (thus it leaves out some of the best European commentators as well as Chinese authors such as the important oral historian and journalist Sang Ye).

Chapter 1

1. For further information on Confucius and other early thinkers discussed in this section, see Benjamin I. Schwartz, *The World of Thought in Ancient China* (Cambridge, MA: Harvard University Press, 1985); the bibliography of this masterful synthetic work will lead the interested reader to good translations of the relevant primary texts; see also, for translated excerpts of key philosophers, Wm. Theodore de Bary et al., eds., *Source of Chinese Tradition*, Volume I, 2nd ed. (New York: Columbia University Press, 2000).

2. On the origin of fortune cookies, see Jennifer 8. Lee, "Solving a Riddle Wrapped in a Mystery inside a Cookie," *New York Times*, January 16, 2008, http://www.nytimes.com/2008/01/16/dining/16fort.html?pagewanted=1&_r=1&em&en=e&ex=1200632400 (accessed July 18, 2012).

3. Lionel M. Jensen, *Manufacturing Confucianism* (Durham, NC: Duke University Press, 1997).

4. On misconceptions about the Great Wall, see Arthur Waldron, *The Great Wall of China: From History to Myth* (Cambridge: Cambridge University Press, 1992).

5. K. E. Brashier, ed., *The First Emperor: Selections from the Grand Historian* (Oxford: Oxford University Press, 2009).

6. For background on the New Culture movement and relevant citations, see Chow Tse-tsung, *The May Fourth Movement: Intellectual Revolution in Modern China* (Cambridge, MA: Harvard University Press, 1960), and Rana Mitter, *A Bitter Revolution: China's Struggle with the Modern World* (Oxford: Oxford University Press, 2004).

7. This language shows up in many places; see, for example, the main English-language website of the Chinese government: http://english.gov.cn/2005–08/06/content_20912.htm (accessed August 6, 2012).

8. Lionel M. Jensen, "Culture Industry, Power, and the Spectacle of China's 'Confucius Institutes,'" in Timothy B. Weston and Lionel M. Jensen, eds., *China in and beyond the Headlines* (Lanham, MD: Rowman and Littlefield, 2012), pp. 271–299, quote from p. 283.

9. I am someone who feels that considerable skepticism and caution is needed when dealing with Confucius Institutes, and that universities should be very careful not to allow anything to happen that will compromise their complete autonomy in fostering free debate regarding China. It is worth noting, however, that some campus talks promoting the first edition of this book, though arranged initially by other units, were supported by funds from Confucius Institutes. After learning of this, I made a point of beginning such presentations by reading sections from the book that emphasized that Confucius had not always been venerated in China and that the Chinese Communist Party had in the past carried out anti-Confucius campaigns. Representatives of Confucius Institutes present at these events never complained, and in fact they

sometimes made a point of saying how much they had enjoyed the talk.

10. Yu Dan, *Confucius from the Heart: Ancient Wisdom for the Modern World* (London: MacMillan, 2009).
11. Andrew Jacobs, "Confucius Statue Vanishes near Tiananmen Square," *New York Times*, April 22, 2011, http://www.nytimes.com/2011/04/23/world/asia/23confucius.html (accessed July 19, 2012).
12. Kenneth L. Pomeranz, *The Great Divergence: China, Europe, and the Making of the Modern World Economy* (Princeton, NJ: Princeton University Press, 2000).

Chapter 2

1. Li Xueqin, *Eastern Zhou and Qin Civilizations* (New Haven, CT: Yale University Press, 1985), pp. 12–15.
2. John King Fairbank and Merle Goldman, *China: A New History* (Cambridge, MA: Belknap Press of Harvard University Press, 1998), p. 59.
3. In *1421: The Year China Discovered America* (New York: William Morrow, 2003), Gavin Menzies claims that Zheng He circumnavigated the globe and reached the Americas decades before Christopher Columbus did. For a more conservative account of Zheng He's voyages, see Louise Levathes, *When China Ruled the Seas: The Treasure Fleet of the Dragon Throne, 1405–1433* (New York: Simon and Schuster, 1994).
4. Peter Ward Fay, *The Opium War, 1840–1842* (Chapel Hill: University of North Carolina Press, 1975); and James Polachek, *The Inner Opium War* (Cambridge, MA: Council on East Asian Studies, Harvard University, 1992).
5. Susan Naquin, *Millenarian Rebellion in China: The Eight Trigrams Uprising of 1813* (New Haven, CT: Yale University Press, 1976).
6. Daniel Overmyer, *Folk Buddhist Religion: Dissenting Sects in Late Imperial China* (Cambridge, MA: Harvard University Press, 1976).
7. Fairbank and Goldman, *China: A New History*, pp. 189–191.
8. Henrietta Harrison, *The Making of the Republican Citizen: Political Ceremonies and Symbols in China, 1911–1929* (Oxford: Oxford University Press, 2000).
9. Harrison Salisbury, *The New Emperors: China in the Era of Mao and Deng* (New York: Avon Books, 1992).
10. John Garnaut, "A Family Affair," *Foreign Policy*, May 30, 2012, http://www.foreignpolicy.com/articles/2012/05/30/a_family_affair (accessed August 6, 2012). Garnaut has written extensively on China's princelings; he has published one short e-book, *The Rise and Fall of the House of Bo* (Penguin, 2012), and is preparing a longer book on the topic.

Chapter 3

1. Marie-Claire Bergère, *Sun Yat-sen*, translated from the French by Janet Lloyd (Stanford, CA: Stanford University Press, 1998).
2. James E. Sheridan, *China in Disintegration: The Republican Period in Chinese History, 1912–1949* (New York: Free Press, 1975).
3. Rana Mitter, *A Bitter Revolution: China's Struggle with the Modern World* (Oxford: Oxford University Press, 2004).
4. The best recent English-language collection of his work is Julia Lovell, trans., *The Real Story of Ah-Q and Other Tales of China: The Complete Fiction of Lu Xun* (New York: Penguin, 2010).
5. For a fictionalized reference to Lu Xun's elevated status in Mao's China, see "Lu Xun," a story in Yu Hua's collection *China in Ten Words* (New York: Pantheon Books, 2011).
6. Arif Dirlik, *The Origins of Chinese Communism* (Oxford: Oxford University Press, 1989).
7. Richard Rigby, *The May Thirtieth Movement: Events and Themes* (Canberra: Australia National University Press, 1980).
8. Donald Jordan, *The Northern Expedition: China's National Revolution of 1926–1928* (Honolulu: University of Hawaii Press, 1976); and, for the Workers' Uprisings, see Elizabeth J. Perry, *Shanghai on Strike: The Politics of Chinese Labor* (Stanford, CA: Stanford University Press, 1993).
9. Edgar Snow, *Red Star over China* (1938; repr., New York: Grove Press, 1968).
10. John King Fairbank and Merle Goldman, *China: A New History* (Cambridge, MA: Belknap Press of Harvard University Press, 1998), p. 305; R. Keith Schoppa, *Revolution and Its Past: Identities and Change in Modern Chinese History* (Upper Saddle River, NJ: Prentice Hall, 2002), p. 235.
11. Benjamin Yang, *From Revolution to Politics: Chinese Communists on the Long March* (Boulder, CO: Westview, 1990).
12. Schoppa, *Revolution and Its Past*, p. 257.
13. Suzanne Pepper, *Civil War in China: The Political Struggle, 1945–1949* (Berkeley: University of California Press, 1978).
14. Quotation by Premiere Zhou Enlai (Chou En-lai), from John Gardner, "The Wu-fan Campaign in Shanghai," in A. Doak Barnett, ed., *Chinese Communist Politics in Action* (Seattle: University of Washington Press, 1969), p. 477.
15. Jonathan D. Spence, *The Search for Modern China*, 2nd ed. (New York: Norton, 1999), pp. 498–513.
16. Susan Glosser, *Chinese Visions of Family and State, 1915–1953* (Berkeley: University of California Press, 2003).
17. Gail Hershatter, *The Gender of Memory: Rural Women and China's Collective Past* (Berkeley: University of California Press, 2011), chap. 7.
18. Mark Selden, ed., *The People's Republic of China: A Documentary History of Revolutionary Change* (New York: Monthly Review Press, 1979), p. 213.

19. Spence, *The Search for Modern China*, p. 553; and Carl Riskin, "Seven Questions about the Chinese Famine of 1959–61," *China Economic Review* 9, no. 2 (1998), pp. 111–124.

20. For more on the "dragon lady" trope in Chinese history, see Paul French, "Tale of the Dragon Lady," *Foreign Policy*, June 26, 2012, http://www.foreignpolicy.com/articles/2012/06/26/tale_of_the_dragon_lady (accessed November 16, 2012). Bo Xilai's wife, Gu Kailai, has frequently been cast in a similar light since he was purged from power and she was arrested for murder in 2012.

21. Jung Chang and Jon Halliday, *Mao: The Unknown Story* (New York: Knopf, 2005).

22. "Mao References in Anti-Japan Protests a Concern for Chinese Authorities," *Asahi Shimbun*, September 18, 2012, http://ajw.asahi.com/article/asia/china/AJ201209180053 (accessed November 12, 2012).

Chapter 4

1. For extensive galleries of PRC propaganda posters, see http://chineseposters.net (accessed August 13, 2012).

2. Ezra F. Vogel, *Deng Xiaoping and the Transformation of China* (Harvard, MA: Belknap Press of Harvard University Press, 2011).

3. George Black and Robin Munro, *Black Hands of Beijing: Lives of Defiance in China's Democracy Movement* (New York: John Wiley, 1993).

4. For the recent rediscovery of "The Communist Manifesto" as a text that has prescient things to say about globalization, and citations to comments on this score by people such as Thomas Friedman, who is not, by any means, associated with the Far Left, see "Afterword: Is the Manifesto Still Relevant?" in Philip Gaster, ed., *The Communist Manifesto: A Road Map to History's Most Important Political Document* (Chicago: Haymarket, 2005).

5. See, for example, Edward Friedman and Barrett L. McCormick, eds., *What If China Doesn't Democratize?* (Armonk, NY: M. E. Sharpe, 2000); and Bruce Dickson, *China's Red Capitalists: The Party, Entrepreneurs, and Prospects for Political Change* (Cambridge: Cambridge University Press, 2003).

6. Julia Lovell, *The Opium War: Drugs, Dreams and the Making of China* (London: Picador, 2011) contains an extended discussion of the post-1989 patriotic education movement.

7. For a typical recent case in point, see "China Dismisses Local Leaders after Angry Protest," a July 25, 2009, Associated Press report http://www.guardian.co.uk/world/feedarticle/8625966 (accessed November 13, 2012).

8. Kevin J. O'Brien, "Rural Protest," *Journal of Democracy* 20, no. 3 (July 2009), pp. 25–28.

9. David Ownby, "China's War against Itself," *New York Times*, February 15, 2001, http://www.nytimes.com/2001/02/15/opinion/

china-s-war-against-itself.html (accessed November 13, 2012). Ownby ends with the claim that the Falun Gong's "evocation of a different vision of Chinese tradition and its contemporary value is now so threatening to the state and party because it denies them the sole right to define the meaning of Chinese nationalism, and perhaps of Chineseness." See also Ownby's book *Falun Gong and the Future of China* (New York: Oxford University Press, 2008).

10. Louisa Lim and Jeffrey Wasserstrom, "The Gray Zone: How Chinese Writers Elude Censors," *New York Times,* June 15, 2012, http://www.nytimes.com/2012/06/17/books/review/how-chinese-writers-elude-censors.html?pagewanted=all (accessed August 22, 2012).

11. For a pair of thoughtful but often diametrically opposed assessments of Mo's writing and qualifications for winning the Nobel Prize, each by a respected specialist in Chinese literature, see Sabina Knight's responses to my queries in this interview I did with her, "China's Latest Laureate: Chinese Lit Scholar Answers Questions about Mo Yan," *Los Angeles Review of Books,* October 12, 2012, http://lareviewofbooks.org/article.php?id=1003 (accessed December 11, 2012); and Perry Link, "Does This Writer Deserve the Prize?," *New York Review of Books,* December 6, 2012, http://www.nybooks.com/articles/archives/2012/dec/06/mo-yan-nobel-prize/?pagination=false (accessed December 11, 2012).

12. Perry Link, "Liu Xiaobo's Empty Chair," *New York Review of Books* blog, December 13, 2010, http://www.nybooks.com/blogs/nyrblog/2010/dec/13/nobel-peace-prize-ceremony-liu-xiaobo/ (accessed August 22, 2012).

13. Maura Elizabeth Cunningham and Jeffrey N. Wasserstrom, "Authoritarianism: There's an App for That," *Chinese Journal of Communication* 5, no. 1 (March 2012), pp. 43–48.

14. The first English-language discussion of "The Great Firewall" metaphor I know of appeared in an important early analysis of the Chinese Internet by Geremie R. Barmé and Sang Ye, "The Great Firewall of China," *Wired* 5, no. 6 (June 1997), pp. 138–150, http://www.wired.com/wired/archive/5.06/china_pr.html (accessed November 13, 2012).

15. See, for example, Andrew Leonard, "Tiananmen's Bloody Lessons for Tehran," posted at the Salon.com blogsite "How the World Works," June 19, 2009, http://www.salon.com/tech/htww/2009/06/19/tiananmen_and_tehran; and Tony Karon, "Iran: Four Ways the Crisis May Resolve," *Time,* June 18, 2009, http://www.time.com/time/world/article/0,8599,1905356,00.html (accessed November 13, 2012). I am grateful to Xiao Qiang for clarifying for me some of the similarities between Chinese and Iranian efforts to control the Internet—and stressing the point of the lesser sophistication and comparative slowness of the moves typically made by the authorities in Tehran as opposed to their counterparts in Beijing.

16. On the overlapping uses of and differences between the terms "Great Firewall" and "Net Nanny," see ULN (a pseudonym for a

blogger who describes himself or herself simply as a "foreigner living happily in Shanghai"), "China's Internet Censorship Explained," posted on the blogsite Chinayouren: Of China Changing the World, January 22, 2009, http://chinayouren.com/en/2009/01/22/1334 (accessed November 13, 2012). Many relevant discussions of the phenomena can also be found at the following websites: RConversation (http://rconversation.blogs.com), Danwei (http://www.danwei.com), China Digital Times (http://chinadigitaltimes.net/), and the Hong Kong–based China Media Project (http://cmp.hku.hk/).

17. See the AFP newswire story, "One-Child Policy Debate Reignited in China," http://www.google.com/hostednews/afp/article/ALeq M5jTNZgyU-1RdjeMoShUkmCnY3CdAw (accessed November 13, 2012).

18. For a lively discussion of the "period police," see Lijia Zhang's excellent memoir *"Socialism Is Great!": A Worker's Memoir of the New China* (New York: Atlas, 2008).

19. Mara Hvistendahl, *Unnatural Selection: Choosing Boys over Girls, and the Consequences of a World Full of Men* (New York: PublicAffairs, 2011).

20. On the "One-Child Policy," see Tyrene White, *China's Longest Campaign* (Ithaca, NY: Cornell University Press, 2006); Susan Greenhalgh, *Just One Child: Science and Policy in Deng's China* (Berkeley: University of California Press, 2008); and Wasserstrom, "Resistance to the One-Child Family," *Modern China* 10, no. 3 (July 1984), pp. 345–374.

21. On just how tightly connected the worlds of industry and government can become in contemporary China, consider this summary that Kenneth Pomeranz provides of the blurring of lines between state and private actors in the Three Gorges Dam project: "While this organization [into parent and subsidiary companies that are given control over different parts of the Chinese government's, and indeed the world's, biggest hydraulic project] allows dam-builders to take advantage of private capital markets and corporate organization, their links to the state remain crucial. Huaneng Power Group, which holds development rights for the Lancang (Upper Mekong), was until recently headed by Li Xiaopeng, son of former Premier (and chief advocate of the Three Gorges project) Li Peng. (The younger Li, who like so many other Chinese leaders has a background in engineering, has since moved on to become deputy governor of Shanxi, with responsibility for industry and coal mining.) His sister, Li Xiaolin, is the CEO of Huaneng's most important subsidiary, China Power International Development Ltd. (a Hong Kong corporation)." Kenneth Pomeranz, "The Great Himalayan Watershed," *New Left Review* 58 (July/August 2009), pp. 5–39.

22. Minxin Pei, "The Dark Side of China's Rise," *Foreign Policy*, March/April 2006, http://www.foreignpolicy.com/articles/2006/02/17/the_dark_side_of_chinas_rise (accessed November 13, 2012), makes

the case for using the concept of "crony capitalism" to think about China, but also describes it as a "neo-Leninist" state.

23. For an early use of "Market-Leninism," see Nicholas Kristof, "China Sees 'Market-Leninism' as Way to Future," *New York Times*, September 6, 1993. Several people have used and given particular spins to the term "Capitalism with Chinese Characteristics" over the years. It has been featured, for example, in the name of an essay by Shawn Breslin, "Capitalism with Chinese Characteristics: The Public, the Private and the International," Murdoch University Asia Research Centre, Working Paper 104 (August 2004), and then in the title of a conference that Scott Kennedy convened at Indiana University, "Capitalism with Chinese Characteristics: China's Political Economy in Comparative and Theoretical Perspectives" (May 19–20, 2006); and after that, it made its appearance on a book jacket, with the publication of Yasheng Huang's *Capitalism with Chinese Characteristics: Entrepreneurship and the State* (Cambridge: Cambridge University Press, 2008).

24. Pallavi Aiyar, "Urumqi Is Not Too Different from Godhra," *Business Standard*, July 16, 2009, http://www.business-standard.com/india/news/pallavi-aiyar-urumqi-is-not-too-differentgodhra/364008 (accessed February 19, 2013).

Chapter 5

1. The classic account of this phenomenon remains Harold Isaacs, *Scratches on Our Minds: American Views of China and India* (Armonk, NY: M. E. Sharpe, 1997), the reissue of a work first published in 1958; introductions to later editions bring the story up to 1980; see also Jonathan D. Spence, *The Chan's Great Continent: China in Western Minds* (New York: W. W. Norton, 1999); and, for an excellent selection of primary sources, Colin Mackerras, *Sinophiles and Sinophobes: Western Views on China* (New York: Oxford University Press, 2001).

2. Ethan Gutman, "A Tale of the New China: What I Saw at the American Embassy in Beijing," *Weekly Standard*, May 24, 1999, p. 23; the author writes of feeling "heady and faint just for being there [in Beijing]: the capital of the next century's Superpower, the center of the world for a day, its youth, Borg-like in their unified loathing of our flag and our little plot." (This last word refers to the fact that there was a widespread assumption in China then, as there still is, that the bombing of the Belgrade embassy had been intentional, not a mistake.) The same author invokes the sci-fi notion of the "Chinese Borg" again in "Who Lost China's Internet?," *Weekly Standard*, February 25, 2002, p. 24.

3. See, for example, Jeffrey N. Wasserstrom, "Student Protests in Fin-de-Siècle China," *New Left Review* 237 (September/October 1999), pp. 52–76.

4. A fascinating discussion of the variation within the category of "Han," which focuses on one specific group, can be found in Sara L. Friedman, "Embodying Civility: Civilizing Processes and Symbolic Citizenship in Southeastern China," *Journal of Asian Studies* 63, no. 3 (August 2004), pp. 687–718.

5. On the wide variety of foot-binding practices, see Dorothy Ko, *Cinderella's Sisters: A Revisionist History of Footbinding* (Berkeley: University of California Press, 2007).

6. For the names containing radicals linked to animals that Han Chinese have used to refer to ethnic groups imagined to be less "civilized," see Dru Gladney, *Dislocating China: Reflections on Muslims, Minorities, and Other Subaltern Subjects* (London: C. Hurst, 2004), p. 35. For a similar process, involving prejudice against Han migrants to the city who are seen as inferior and referred to by some locals as "Subei swine," for example, see Emily Honig, *Creating Chinese Ethnicity: Subei People in Shanghai, 1850–1980* (New Haven, CT: Yale University Press, 1992).

7. Carl Haub, "China Releases First 2010 Census Results," *Population Reference Bureau*, May 2011, http://www.prb.org/Articles/2011/china-census-results.aspx (accessed August 26, 2012).

8. Interesting recent nods to *Brave New World's* relevance for thinking about today's PRC, which sometimes present it as a valuable supplement to or substitute for treatments of China as an Orwellian "Big Brother" state, include Howard W. French, "Letter from China: What If Beijing Is Right?" *New York Times*, November 2, 2007, http://www.nytimes.com/2007/11/02/world/asia/02iht-letter.1.8162318.html?pagewanted=1&_r=1 (accessed August 26, 2012); Rana Mitter, *Modern China: A Very Short Introduction* (Oxford: Oxford University Press, 2007); Marcus Anthony, "The New China: Big Brother, Brave New World, or Harmonious Society?" *Journal of Future Studies* 11, no. 4 (May 2007), pp. 15–40, http://www.scribd.com/doc/16999747/China-Big-Brother-Brave-New-World-or-Harmonious-Society (accessed August 26, 2012); and the Jeremy Goldkorn article quoted from below. My first publication to discuss the relative value of these two analogies was "China's Brave New World," *Current History* 102, no. 665 (September 2003), pp. 266–269; an expanded version of that piece served as the title chapter for my *China's Brave New World—And Other Tales for Global Times* (Bloomington: Indiana University Press, 2007), pp. 125–132. I make no claim to have been the first to suggest that Huxley as well as Orwell might provide a useful lens through which to view Chinese phenomena, including the culture of distraction associated with online gaming (something I mention in my 2003 essay), and in fact, back in 1997, in the *Wired* article on Internet censorship alluded to above, "The Great Firewall of China," Geremie Barmé and Sang Ye used the phrase "Brave New Net" as the subtitle for one of their subsections.

9. For more on this letter, see Wasserstrom, *China's Brave New World*, p. 125.

10. For early and recent examples of this argument, see John J. Thacik, "China's Orwellian Internet," Heritage Foundation Backgrounder #1806 (October 8, 2004), http://www.heritage.org/research/asiaandthepacific/bg1806.cfm (accessed August 26, 2012); and William Pesek, "Web Porn Won't Hurt China as Much as Orwell Will," Bloomberg News, June 22, 2009, http://www.bloomberg.com/apps/news?pid=20601039&sid=aIHVyrLaYtiQ (accessed August 26, 2012).

11. Jeremy Goldkorn, "Dystopia and Censorship," Danwei website, August 27, 2009, http://www.danwei.org/internet_culture/dystopia_and_censorship.php (accessed August 26, 2012). This piece is framed around an excerpt from an important August 26, 2009, op-ed of his that appeared in the *Daily Telegraph*, "China's Internet, the Wild, Wild East," but it ran, as he notes, without the final line quoted above that alluded to Orwell and Huxley, an omission he rectified in the version that he posted at the URL provided above.

12. I had never thought of the parallels between Tibet and Hawaii until a conversation with the political scientist Elizabeth J. Perry, in which she mentioned, in passing, that she had found this analogy a useful one to use when Americans asked her about the March 2008 conflicts. She did not elaborate on the idea, but it immediately struck me as a very fitting one—not least because more than a few Han Chinese, however they feel about the political side of the issue, now think of Tibet as a travel destination, if one wants to encounter an "exotic" culture in a stunning natural setting.

Chapter 6

1. Leslie T. Chang, *Factory Girls: From Village to City in a Changing China* (New York: Spiegel & Grau, 2008), p. 12.

2. Edward Wong, "Ending Congress, China Presents New Leadership Headed by Xi Jinping," *New York Times*, November 14, 2012, http://www.nytimes.com/2012/11/15/world/asia/communists-conclude-party-congress-in-china.html?_r=0 (accessed November 16, 2012).

3. For a smart, accessibly written scholarly account, see Stanley Rosen, "Contemporary Chinese Youth and the State," *Journal of Asian Studies* 68, no. 2 (May 2009), pp. 359–369; for state-of-the-art journalism on the same subject, see Evan Osnos, "Angry Youth," *New Yorker*, July 28, 2008, http://www.newyorker.com/reporting/2008/07/28/080728fa_fact_osnos (accessed November 15, 2012). Anti-Japanese protests in August and September 2012 once again led to a slew of commentaries on the complexities of Chinese nationalism; one of the most intriguing is Helen Gao, "Diaoyu in Our Heart: The Revealing Contradictions of Chinese Nationalism," *The Atlantic*, August 22, 2012, http://www.theatlantic.com/international/archive/2012/08/diaoyu-in-our-heart-the-revealing-contradictions-of-chinese-nationalism/261422/ (accessed November 16, 2012).

4. See Suisheng Zhao, "China's Pragmatic Nationalism: Is It Manageable?" *Washington Quarterly* 29, no. 1 (Winter 2005–2006), pp. 131–144; and Dune Lawrence, "Carrefour Boycott Has China Reining in Supporters," Bloomberg News, April 29, 2008, http://www.bloomberg.com/apps/news?pid=newsarchive&sid=aw1fsXd RYEvU&refer=asia (accessed November 16, 2012).

5. On this issue, see Elizabeth J. Perry and Sebastian Heilmann, eds., *Mao's Invisible Hand: The Political Foundations of Adaptive Governance in China* (Cambridge, MA: Harvard University Press, 2011).

6. Chen Xin and Zhi Yun, "China's Coal Mines Still Risky," *China Daily*, August 25, 2012, http://www.chinadaily.com.cn/china/2012–08/25/content_15705033.htm (accessed November 16, 2012).

7. Kenneth Pomeranz, "The Great Himalayan Watershed," *New Left Review* 58 (July/August 2009), pp. 5–39.

8. Ananth Krishnan, "Corruption, Reforms Dominate China's Communist Party Meet Opener," *The Hindu*, November 8, 2012, http://www.thehindu.com/news/international/hu-talks-tough-on-corruption-as-china-opens-transition-congress/article4076505.ece (accessed November 16, 2012).

9. "Xi Jinping Millionaire Relations Reveal Fortunes of Elite," Bloomberg News, June 29, 2012, http://www.bloomberg.com/news/2012–06–29/xi-jinping-millionaire-relations-reveal-fortunes-of-elite.html (accessed November 16, 2012); David Barboza, "Billions in Hidden Riches for Family of Chinese Leader," *New York Times*, October 25, 2012, http://www.nytimes.com/2012/10/26/business/global/family-of-wen-jia-bao-holds-a-hidden-fortune-in-china.html (accessed November 16, 2012).

10. Christina Larson, "Apocalypse Mao," *Foreign Policy*, November 15, 2012, http://www.foreignpolicy.com/articles/2012/11/15/apocalypse_mao (accessed November 16, 2012).

11. After finishing work on the first edition of this book, I saw an advance copy of Bruce Cummings's *Dominion from Sea to Sea: Pacific Ascendancy and American Power* (New Haven, CT: Yale University Press, 2009), which is primarily about the United States, as its title suggests, but ends with comments about the desirability of embracing the heretical notion that the two countries have much in common. If what I have to say about US–China similarities here whets their appetite to learn more about the theme, I encourage readers to pick up a copy of his powerful take on US foreign policy.

12. See Pankaj Mishra, "At War with the Utopia of Modernity," *Guardian*, March 22, 2008, http://www.guardian.co.uk/commentisfree/2008/mar/22/tibet.china1 (accessed November 16, 2012).

13. Peter Hessler, "China's Instant Cities," *National Geographic*, June 2007, http://ngm.nationalgeographic.com/2007/06/instant-cities/hessler-text (accessed November 16, 2012).

14. Stephen Mihm, "A Nation of Outlaws," in Kate Merkel-Hess et al., *China in 2008: A Year of Great Significance* (Lanham, MD: Rowman & Littlefield, 2009).

15. David Biello, "Can Coal and Clean Air Co-exist in China?" *Scientific American*, August 4, 2008, http://www.scientificamerican. com/article.cfm?id=can-coal-and-clean-air-coexist-china (accessed November 16, 2012).

16. "America's and Japan's Olympic Debuts: Lessons for Beijing 2008 (and the Tibet Controversy)," *Japan Focus* #2754, 2008, http://www. japanfocus.org/-Susan-Brownell/2754 (accessed November 16, 2012).

17. Mihm, "Nation of Outlaws," p. 278.

FURTHER READING

Part I: General

Broad college surveys of Chinese history used to be dubbed "Yao to Mao" courses, playing upon the names of one of the legendary sage kings of the prerecorded past and the first paramount leader of the People's Republic of China. (Now, of course, one could speak of a follow-up "Mao to Yao" class; it would go from the death of Mao in 1976 up to the era of the basketball star Yao Ming. Yao first made headlines by scoring points and blocking shots in Texas sports arenas, went on to play a role in the Opening Ceremonies of the 2008 Olympics, and generated renewed media buzz in 2012 for welcoming Jeremy Lin, the Chinese-American sports sensation, to his former team, the Houston Rockets, and making a high-profile goodwill trip to Africa.) For useful, accessibly written general overviews that take you from "Yao to Mao," good places to turn include Patricia Ebrey's *The Cambridge Illustrated History of China* (Cambridge University Press, 1999) and John K. Fairbank and Merle Goldman, *China: A New History* (Harvard University Press, 1998). Two valuable works with a large but not quite as large temporal sweep are Charles Hucker, *China to 1850: A Short History* (Stanford University Press, 1978), a model of conciseness, and Jonathan Spence, *The Search for Modern China*, third edition (W. W. Norton, 2013), a model of fluent and erudite narrative prose that begins with the rise to power of the Qing Dynasty (1644–1912). All of these publications, except for the final one, appeared toward the end of the last century, and hence, while very valuable, they do not take on board the very latest findings of academic specialists. Below, however, readers will find many specialized works that were published in the 21st century and are informed by the very latest scholarship.

Chapter 1

One of the best general introductions to the ideas of Confucius, Mencius, and competing philosophers of their eras remains Benjamin Schwartz, *The World of Thought in Ancient China* (Harvard University Press, 1985). For a collection of translations of selected works by these thinkers, all carefully introduced, see Wm. Theodore de Bary and Irene Bloom, editors, *Sources of Chinese Tradition, Volume 1: From Earliest Times to 1600* (Columbia University Press, 1999). Arthur Waley's *Three Ways of Thought in Ancient China* (Stanford University Press, 1939) remains a good work to turn to for getting a basic appreciation of the similarities and differences between the worldviews of Mencius and the Daoists and Legalists (referred to by Waley as "Realists") who lived at the same time as he did or a century or so before or after him; it is filled with translations of particularly engaging passages (and sometimes, especially in the case of the Daoist Zhuang Zi, ones that are amusing as well as illuminating). For background on the First Emperor and his posthumous reputations, see K. E. Brashier's excellent introduction to Sima Qian, *The First Emperor: Selections from the Historical Records*, translated by Raymond Dawson (Oxford University Press, 2007). On the complex process by which the ideas of Confucius and his followers evolved into something known as "Confucianism," see Lionel M. Jensen, *Manufacturing Confucianism: Chinese Traditions and Universal Civilization* (Duke University Press, 1997). For background on the veneration of Confucius in the past and the return of temples and statues honoring him in recent years, see Julia K. Murray, "'Idols' in the Temple: Icons and the Cult of Confucius," *Journal of Asian Studies* 68, no. 2 (2009), pp. 371–411. For a more positive assessment of the meaning of the revival of interest in Confucius and his thought than I provide, see Daniel A. Bell, *China's New Confucianism* (Princeton University Press, 2008); for a valuable, appreciative yet critical look at this book, see Timothy Cheek, "The Karaoke Classics: A View from Inside China's Confucian Revival," *Literary Review of Canada*, November 2008, http://reviewcanada.ca/reviews/2008/11/01/the-karaoke-classics/. And for a variety of short takes on the Opening Ceremonies of the Beijing Games, including in some cases analysis of the allusions to Confucius made during it, see the relevant essays by Geremie R. Barmé, Lee Haiyan, and others in Kate Merkel-Hess, Kenneth L. Pomeranz, and Jeffrey N. Wasserstrom, editors, *China in 2008: A Year of Great Significance* (Rowman and Littlefield, 2009; hereafter *China in 2008*). For varied takes on Chinese democratic traditions (and the related theme of Chinese human rights traditions), see Andrew J. Nathan, *Chinese Democracy* (University of California Press, 1986); Marina Svensson, *Debating Human Rights in China* (Rowman and Littlefield, 2002); and Joseph W. Esherick and Jeffrey N. Wasserstrom, "Acting Out Democracy: Political Theater in Modern China," *Journal of Asian Studies*, November 1990, pp. 835–865.

Chapter 2

Readers looking for scholarly but accessible surveys of specific dynasties, which are completely up-to-date in terms of the academic studies that inform them, can turn to the Harvard University Press series edited by Timothy Brook. The series is called "History of Imperial China," and the volumes in this important undertaking include two by Mark Lewis, *The Early Chinese Empires: Qin and Han* (2007) and *China's Cosmopolitan Empire: The Tang Dynasty* (2009); Dieter Kuhn, *The Age of Confucian Rule: The Song Transformation of China* (2009); Timothy Brook, *The Troubled Empire: China in the Yuan and Ming Dynasties* (2010); and William T. Rowe, *China's Last Empire: The Great Qing* (2009). For an overview of late imperial China, see Frederic E. Wakeman Jr., *The Fall of Imperial China* (Free Press, 1975). Engaging recent accounts of mid-19th-century events include Julia Lovell, *The Opium War: Drugs, Dreams and the Making of China* (Picador, 2011); Robert Bickers, *The Scramble for China: Foreign Devils in the Qing Empire, 1832–1914* (Penguin, 2011); and Stephen R. Platt, *Autumn in the Heavenly Kingdom: China, The West and the Epic Story of the Taiping Civil War* (Knopf, 2012)—a trio of books introduced, compared, and contrasted in Maura Elizabeth Cunningham, "Forgetting and Remembering: New Books on China and the West in the Nineteenth Century," *World History Connected*, October 2012, http://worldhistoryconnected.press.illinois.edu/9.3/br_cunningham.html. On the Boxers, see Joseph W. Esherick, *The Origins of the Boxer Uprising* (University of California Press, 1988); Paul A. Cohen, *History in Three Keys: The Boxers as History, Myth, and Experience* (Columbia University Press, 1997); and Robert Bickers and R. G. Tiedemann, editors, *The Boxers, China, and the World* (Rowman and Littlefield, 2007). For similarities and differences between Chinese imperial rulers and the leaders of the Communist Party, along with many other subjects of interest, see Geremie R. Barmé, *The Forbidden City* (Profile Books, 2008).

Chapter 3

There are many valuable books that cover some or all of the events and people discussed in this section, and that provide information that is more detailed than could be provided here, yet are still very accessibly written. Most also contain footnotes, bibliographical essays, or both that will point the reader to still more specialized studies. See, for example, Rana Mitter, *A Bitter Revolution: China's Struggle with the Modern World* (Oxford University Press, 2005), which is particularly strong on the legacy of the May 4th Movement; Jonathan Fenby, *The Penguin History of Modern China: The Fall and Rise of a Great Power, 1850–2009* (Penguin, 2008), which is especially useful for its handling of political events involving the Nationalist Party and Communist

Party and the personalities of leaders; John Gittings, *The Changing Face of China* (Oxford University Press, 2006), which is very effective in tracing events of the Mao years (1949–1976); Peter Zarrow, *China in War and Revolution, 1895–1949* (Routledge, 2005), which handles intellectual trends in a sophisticated manner; and Pamela Crossley, *The Wobbling Pivot, China since 1800: An Interpretive History* (Wiley, 2010), which has a distinctive focus on the relationship between central authorities and local communities.

For the lives and times of the two main Nationalist leaders, see Marie-Claire Bergère, *Sun Yat-sen* (Stanford University Press, 2000) and Jay Taylor, *The Generalissimo: Chiang Kai-shek and the Struggle for Modern China* (Harvard University Press, 2009). The literature on Mao is enormous. The most up-to-date comprehensive biography is Alexander V. Pantsov and Steven I. Levine, *Mao: The Real Story* (Simon and Schuster, 2012). Two valuable short books are Timothy Cheek's *Mao Zedong and the Chinese Revolutions: A Brief History with Documents* (Bedford, 2002), which includes translations of some of the leader's most significant tracts, and Rebecca Karl's *Mao Zedong and China in the Twentieth-Century World* (Duke University Press, 2010). Important essays on various aspects of Mao's life and legacy, written by leading specialists in diverse specific fields, can be found in Timothy Cheek, editor, *A Critical Introduction to Mao* (Cambridge University Press, 2010). For Lu Xun, see *The Real Story of Ah-Q and Other Tales of China: The Complete Fiction of Lu Xun* (Penguin, 2009), which comes with an excellent overview of his life and writings by translator Julia Lovell. For a bottom-up look at the Mao period, see Edward Friedman et al., *Chinese Village, Socialist State* (Yale University Press, 1993); for a sense of what it was like to grow up in the era, see the reminisces in various sections of Yu Hua, *China in Ten Words*, translated by Allan Barr (Pantheon, 2011), and Xueping Zhong et al., *Some of Us: Chinese Women Growing Up in the Mao Era* (Rutgers, 2011); on the Marriage Law, see Susan Glosser, *Chinese Visions of Family and State, 1915–1953* (University of California Press, 2003).

On the lead-up to and playing out of the Cultural Revolution, see Roderick MacFarquhar and Michael Schoenhals, *Mao's Last Revolution* (Harvard University Press, 2006); the powerful documentary film *Morning Sun* (2005) (directed by Carma Hinton and Geremie R. Barmé; the related website is http://www.morningsun.org); and Richard C. Kraus, *The Cultural Revolution: A Very Short Introduction* (Oxford University Press, 2012), which is a marvel of erudite concision. On student actions in China's capital, see Andrew G. Walder, *Fractured Rebellion: The Beijing Red Guard Movement* (Harvard University Press, 2009); for the cultural, artistic, and gendered dimensions of the period, see Harriet Evans and Stephanie Donald, editors, *Picturing Power in the People's Republic of China: Posters of the Cultural Revolution* (Rowman and Littlefield, 1999), a richly illustrated collection of essays; and for violent events in the countryside, see Yang Su, *Collective Killings in Rural China during the Cultural Revolution* (Cambridge University Press, 2011). On the Great Leap Famine, see Yang Jisheng, *Tombstone: The Great Chinese*

Famine, 1958–1962, translated by Stacy Mosher and Guo Jian (FSG, 2012); Zhou Xun, editor, *The Great Famine in China, 1958–1962: A Documentary History* (Yale University Press, 2012); and Frank Dikötter, *Mao's Great Famine* (Bloomsbury, 2010). For Mao's reputation since 1976 and debates about the meaning of his life and deeds, see Geremie R. Barmé, *Shades of Mao: The Posthumous Cult of the Great Leader* (M. E. Sharpe, 1996) and Lin Chun and Gregor Benton, editors, *Was Mao Really a Monster?* (Routledge, 2009).

Part II: General

Some of the best books to turn to in order to get a sense of how China has been changing in recent years and the human side of the country's dramatic transformations are the works of freelance writers and journalists, such as Ian Johnson, Michelle Dammon Loyalka, Zha Jianying, Duncan Hewitt, Leslie T. Chang, Michael Meyer, Peter Hessler, and Sang Ye. Three good books to begin with are Hessler's *Country Driving: A Journey through China from Farm to Factory* (Harper's, 2010); a collection of Sang Ye's Studs Terkel–like interviews with ordinary Chinese from many walks of life that have been brought together and translated superbly by Geremie R. Barmé as *China Candid: The People of the People's Republic of China* (University of California Press, 2006); and Zha's *Tide Players: The Movers and Shakers of a Rising China* (New Press, 2011). See also Angilee Shah and my coedited volume, *Chinese Characters: Profiles of Fast-Changing Lives in a Fast-Changing Land* (University of California Press, 2012), which offers a sampling of short pieces by a diverse array of gifted writers, including several of those mentioned above. A valuable introduction to contemporary Chinese politics and recent US–China relations is provided by Susan Shirk, *China: Fragile Superpower* (Oxford University Press, 2007), while an engaging presentation of basic facts about the country can be found in Stephanie Donald and Robert Benewick, *The State of China Atlas*, revised and updated edition (University of California Press, 2009).

Chapter 4

For general introductions to the post-1976 period, see Richard Baum's *Burying Mao: Chinese Politics in the Era of Deng Xiaoping*, updated edition (Princeton University Press, 1996), which is particularly good on high politics; Timothy Cheek's *Living with Reform: China since 1989* (Zed, 2007), which is good on cultural and intellectual developments; and Ezra Vogel's *Deng Xiaoping and the Transformation of China* (Harvard University Press, 2011), for an account that approaches the period through the prism of the life of its most powerful figure. On Democracy Wall and related events, see Andrew J. Nathan, *Chinese Democracy* (University of California Press, 1986); Merle Goldman, *Sowing the Seeds of Democracy in China: Political Reform in the Deng Xiaoping Decade* (Harvard University Press, 1994); and Geremie R. Barmé and John Minford, editors, *Seeds of Fire: Chinese Voices of Conscience* (Hill and Wang, 1988). On the events and intellectual trends that led up to Tiananmen, see the final chapter of Jeffrey N. Wasserstrom, *Student Protests in Twentieth-Century China: The View from Shanghai* (Stanford University Press, 1991); various chapters in Elizabeth J. Perry and Jeffrey N. Wasserstrom, editors, *Popular Protest and Political Culture in Modern China*, second edition (Westview, 1994); and Perry Link, *Evening Chats in Beijing* (W. W. Norton, 1993).

The literature on Tiananmen itself is enormous (even limiting one's purview to English-language materials, as there are also voluminous publications in Chinese and important studies and document collections in French and other Western languages). A good selection of relevant works is available at http://www.tsquare.tv, a website created to accompany the excellent documentary *The Gate of Heavenly Peace* (1996), directed by Carma Hinton and Richard Gordon. See also Craig Calhoun, *Neither Gods nor Emperors: Students and the Struggle for Democracy in China* (University of California Press, 1997), and Philip J. Cunningham, *Tiananmen Moon: Inside the Chinese Student Uprising of 1989* (Rowman and Littlefield, 2009); for the massacre itself and some key figures in the struggle, George Black and Robin Munro, *Black Hands of Beijing* (Wiley, 1993); for the actions of the army, Timothy Brook, *Quelling the People* (Stanford University Press, 1998); for the writings of participants, Han Minzhu, editor, *Cries for Democracy* (Princeton University Press, 1990) and Geremie R. Barmé and Linda Jaivin, editors, *New Ghosts, Old Dreams* (Crown, 1992); for events outside of Beijing, Jonathan Unger, editor, *The Chinese Democracy Movement: Reports from the Provinces* (M. E. Sharpe, 1991); and for the perspective on the unrest of high-ranking Communist Party officials, Zhao Ziyang, *Prisoner of the State: The Secret Journal of Zhao Ziyang* (Simon and Schuster, 2009), as well as Liang Zhang, compiler, *The Tiananmen Papers* (Public Affairs, 2001).

For the ability of the CCP to remain in power since 1989, and social changes in the intervening years, see Peter Hays Gries and Stanley Rosen, editors, *State and Society in 21st-Century China* (Routledge, 2004), especially the chapter on legitimacy by Vivienne Shue; Elizabeth J. Perry and Mark Selden, editors, *Chinese Society: Change, Conflict and Resistance*, second edition (Routledge, 2003), which is particularly good on protests since Tiananmen; David Shambaugh, *China's Communist Party: Atrophy and Adaptation* (University of California Press, 2008), which shines in illuminating efforts the party made to learn from the fall of other state socialist regimes; Sebastian Heilmann and Elizabeth J. Perry, editors, *Mao's Invisible Hand: The Political Foundations of Adaptive Governance in China* (Harvard University Press, 2011), which reminds us of how ready to experiment the CCP has been throughout its history; Richard McGregor, *The Party: The Secret World of China's Communist Rulers* (Harper, 2010), a work that is strong on the ways that political, business, and military concerns intertwine; and the contributions by Andrew J. Nathan (probably the leading proponent of the "resilient authoritarianism" idea) and others in a special section on China since 1989 included in the July 2009 issue of the *Journal of Democracy*. On Falun Gong, see David Ownby, *Falun Gong and the Future of China* (Oxford University Press, 2008).

On the complex landscape of intellectual life in contemporary China, and the need to think in terms of more than just a simple divide between "dissidents" and apologists for the regime, see the compendium of views showcased in important collections edited by Wang Chaohua, *One China, Many Paths* (Verso, 2005), and by Gloria Davies, *Voicing Concerns* (Rowman and Littlefield, 2001). See also Michael Dutton, *Streetlife China* (Cambridge University Press, 1999); Geremie R. Barmé, *In the Red* (Columbia University Press, 1999), which remains the best overall account of the strategies that artists and intellectuals use to navigate in the gray zone between officially allowed and overtly repressed forms of cultural activities (for a recent account of this issue, see Louisa Lim and my "The Gray Zone: How Chinese Writers Elude Censors," *New York Times*, June 5, 2012); and many posts on *New Yorker* correspondent Evan Osnos's excellent "Letter from China" blog, including "Jia Zhangke and Rebiya Kadeer," at http://www.newyorker.com/online/blogs/evanosnos/2009/07/jia-zhangke-rebiya-kadeer.html.

On Han Han, see the collection of his blog posts selected and translated by Allan Barr and published as *This Generation* (Simon and Schuster, 2012). He and Ai Weiwei are discussed in Geremie Barmé, editor, *Red Rising, Red Eclipse* (Australia National University, 2012), with sample blog posts by each included in the "Voices from the Blogosphere" chapters of that volume. On Mo Yan, see Perry Link, "Does This Writer Deserve the Prize?," *New York Review of Books*, December 6, 2012; and, for a contrasting view, Charles Laughlin, "What Mo Yan's Detractors Get Wrong," ChinaFile (an Asia Society online publication), December 11, 2012, http://www.chinafile.com/what-mo-yan%E2%80%99s-detractors-get-wrong. On Liu Xiaobo, see the collection of his writings edited by Perry Link, Tienchi Martin-Liao, and Liu Xia, working with various translators, *No Enemies, No Hatred: Selected Essays and Poems* (Harvard University Press, 2012), which comes with an extended "Introduction" by Link.

On Chinese birth control campaigns, see Susan Greenhalgh, *Just One Child: Science and Policy in Deng's China* (University of California Press, 2008), and, for a summary, Harriet Evans, "The Little Emperor Grows Selfish," New Statesman, January 1, 2005, http://www.newstatesman.com/200501010012. On the meaning of the Olympics, see Susan Brownell, *Beijing's Games: What the Olympics Mean to China* (Rowman and Littlefield, 2008).

On China–India comparisons, see the insightful writings of Pankaj Mishra (e.g., "It's a Round World After All: India, China, and the Global Economy," *Harper's*, August 2007, pp. 83–88) and Pranab Bardhan (e.g., "India and China: Governance Issues and Development," *Journal of Asian Studies*, May 2009, pp. 347–357), and the many references to similarities and differences between the countries that are included in Pallavi Aiyar,

Smoke and Mirrors: An Experience of China (HarperCollins India, 2008). A wonderfully readable and carefully researched work on Xinjiang is James Millward, *Eurasian Crossroads: A History of Xinjiang* (Columbia University Press, 2007); for a valuable assessment of the July 2009 unrest by the author of that volume, see James Millward, "The Urumqi Unrest Revisited," a posting for "The China Beat" blog, July 29, 2009, http://www.thechinabeat.org/?p=558. See also John Gittings, "China's Uighur Conundrum," *Guardian*, July 7, 2009, http://www.guardian.co.uk/commentisfree/2009/jul/07/uighur-china-xinjiang-urumqi.

For "digital divides" and control of the Internet, see Guobin Yang, *The Power of the Internet in China* (Columbia University Press, 2009) and also Susan Shirk, editor, *Changing Media, Changing China* (Oxford University Press, 2010). Much of the essential writing on these issues, not surprisingly, appears online, in venues such as former CNN Beijing bureau chief and now prominent new media analyst Rebecca MacKinnon's RConversation (http://rconversation.blogs.com), Jeremy Goldkorn's Danwei: Chinese Media, Marketing, Advertising, and Urban Life (http://www.danwei.com), the Berkeley-based China Digital Times (http://chinadigitaltimes.net/), and the Hong Kong–based China Media Project (http://cmp.hku.hk/). More recent sites that track the topic well include ChinaFile (http://www.chinafile.com), The China Story (http://www.thechinastory.org/), and Tea Leaf Nation (http://www.tealeafnation.com).

Chapter 5

For background on US–Chinese interactions and mutual images, see Jonathan Spence, *To Change China: Western Advisers in China* (Penguin, 2002); Harold R. Isaac, *Scratches on Our Minds* (M. E. Sharpe, 1980); David Arkush and Lee Ou-fan Lee, editors, *Land Without Ghosts: Chinese Impressions of America from the Mid-Nineteenth Century to the Present* (University of California Press, 1993); Scott Kennedy, editor, *China Cross-Talk* (Rowman and Littlefield, 2003); David Shambaugh, *Beautiful Imperialist: China Perceives America, 1972–1990* (Princeton University Press, 1993); and Warren G. Cohen, *America's Response to China: A History of Sino-American Relations*, fifth edition (Columbia University Press, 2010). Astute and accessible treatments of many issues dealt with in this chapter can be found in a trio of books edited by Lionel M. Jensen and Timothy B. Weston: *China beyond the Headlines* (Rowman and Littlefield, 2000), *China's Transformations* (Rowman and Littlefield, 2007), and *China in and beyond the Headlines* (Rowman and Littlefield, 2012).

On religion in the PRC, see Yoshiko Ashiwa and David L. Wank, editors, *Making Religion, Making the State: The Politics of Religion in Modern China* (Stanford University Press, 2009); various articles, reviews, and commentaries by Ian Johnson, including "China Gets Religion!" *New York Review of Books*, December 22, 2011; and the materials by Evan Osnos and others that are gathered together on the website for the *Frontline* documentary "Jesus in China," http://www.pbs.org/frontlineworld/

stories/china_705/. On regional and other related divides, see Susan D. Blum and Lionel M. Jensen, editors, *China Off Center: Mapping the Margins of the Middle Kingdom* (University of Hawaii Press, 2002); Rob Gifford, *China Road: A Journey into the Future of a Rising Power* (Random House, 2007); and Li Cheng, "Rediscovering Urban Subcultures: The Contrast between Shanghai and Beijing," *China Journal*, July 1996, pp. 139–153. For ethnic variation, see Ralph Litzinger, *Other Chinas: The Yao and the Politics of National Belonging* (Duke University Press, 2000); Thomas S. Mullaney, "Introducing Critical Han Studies," in the important online periodical *China Heritage Quarterly*, September 2009, http:// www.chinaheritagequarterly.org/scholarship.php?searchterm=019_ han_studies.inc&issue=019; and Sara L. Friedman, *Intimate Politics: Marriage, the Market, and State Power in Southeastern China* (Harvard University Press, 2006), which examines a group classified as "Han" but has a distinctive approach to gender relations. On generational divides, see the lively account in Duncan Hewitt, *Getting Rich First: A Modern Social History* (Pegasus, 2008); Yan Yunxiang, *Private Life under Socialism* (Stanford University Press, 2003) and "Little Emperors or Frail Pragmatists?" *Current History*, September 2006, pp. 255–262; the archives of Alec Ash's now-dormant blog "Six" (http://www.thinksix.net/); and Zachary Mexico, *China Underground* (Soft Skull, 2009).

For further discussion of Orwell and Huxley as guides to the PRC, see my *China's Brave New World—and Other Tales for Global Times* (Indiana University Press, 2007), and my "Hot Dystopic: Orwell and Huxley and China's World's Fair," *Los Angeles Review of Books*, May 20, 2011, http:// lareviewofbooks.org/article.php?id=199&fulltext=1. On the complexities of Tibet, one useful place to start is with Pico Iyer's very sympathetic but nuanced and engaging biography of its spiritual leader in exile, *The Open Road: The Global Journey of the Fourteenth Dalai Lama* (Knopf, 2008), pairing a reading of this book with a look at two insightful reviews that use discussion of it as a starting point for assessing contemporary dilemmas: Robert Barnett, "Thunder from Tibet," *New York Review of Books*, May 29, 2008, http://www.nybooks.com/articles/21391; and Pankaj Mishra, "Holy Man," *New Yorker*, March 31, 2008, http://www. newyorker.com/arts/critics/books/2008/03/31/080331crbo_books_ mishra?currentPage=all. See also the contributions to the section on Tibet in the previously cited Merkel-Hess et al., *China in 2008*.

Chapter 6

Though it may seem odd to include this in a section devoted to "Further Reading," some of the best coverage of all of the issues addressed in this chapter can be found in the 2010–2012 reports by three talented and experienced journalists based in China working for different American public radio programs. The trio I have in mind is Louisa Lim of NPR (most often heard on *Morning Edition*), Mary Kay Magistad of PRI (most often heard on *The World*), and Rob Schmitz of APM (who reports from

Shanghai and other parts of China for *Marketplace*). Fortunately, these reports often have a continued existence online, either in the form of podcasts, transcripts, or both, so that those who miss them when initially broadcast can still benefit from them. Other valuable sources to know about for keeping up with topics addressed here include Tania Branigan's reporting for *The Guardian* (samples of this can be found here: http://www.guardian.co.uk/profile/taniabranigan), the *Wall Street Journal*'s "China Real Time Report" blog (http://blogs.wsj.com/chinarealtime/); and Adam Minter's "Shanghai Scrap" blog (http://shanghaiscrap.com/).

For a good introduction to the People's Liberation Army, past and present, see Andrew Scobell, *China's Use of Military Force* (Cambridge University Press, 2003). On the Taiwan issue, see Nancy Bernkopf Tucker, *Strait Talk: United States-Taiwan Relations and the Crisis with China* (Harvard University Press, 2009) and Shelley Rigger, *Why Taiwan Matters: Small Island, Global Powerhouse* (Rowman and Littlefield, 2011). On Hong Kong, while there is an enormous literature on the 1997 transition, a good place to start is with John M. Carroll, *A Concise History of Hong Kong* (Rowman and Littlefield, 2007) and the admittedly idiosyncratic but lively introduction to contemporary life in the former Crown colony provided by Leo Ou-fan Lee, *City Between Worlds: My Hong Kong* (Harvard University Press, 2008). On China's shift from being a country of villages to one of cities, a sampling of recent academic approaches to the topic, with particular attention to comparative themes, is provided in John Logan, editor, *Urban China in Transition* (Wiley, 2008); for a compelling work of reportage that explores the human side of rural-to-urban migration, see Leslie T. Chang, *Factory Girls: From Village to City in a Changing China* (Spiegel and Grau, 2007); see also the important study by Dorothy Solinger, *Contesting Citizenship in Urban China* (University of California Press, 1999), and Michelle Dammon Loyalka's elegantly crafted profiles of migrant workers in Xi'an, *Eating Bitterness: Stories from the Frontline of China Great Urban Migration* (University of California, 2012).

On China's political future and endemic problems such as corruption, some notable writings that fall at different points on the spectrum running from pessimism to optimism include Perry Link and Josh Kurlantzick, "China's Modern Authoritarianism," *Wall Street Journal*, May 25, 2009; Philip P. Pan, *Out of Mao's Shadow: The Struggle for the Soul of a New China* (Simon and Schuster, 2008); John Pomfret, *Chinese Lessons* (Holt, 2006); Ian Johnson, *Wild Grass: Three Stories of Change in Modern China* (Pantheon, 2004); Elizabeth J. Perry and Merle Goldman, editors, *Grassroots Political Reform in Contemporary China* (Harvard University Press, 2007); George J. Gilboy and Benjamin L. Read, "Political and Social Reform in China: Alive and Walking," *Washington Quarterly*, Summer 2008, pp. 143–164; and Barmé, editor, *Red Rising, Red Eclipse*.

On the 18th Party Congress, the Bo Xilai scandal, and related 2012 events, see the "Changing of the Guard" series published by the *New York Times* (relevant articles are gathered together at http://

topics.nytimes.com/top/features/timestopics/series/changing_of_the_ guard/index.html) and the coverage of this subject throughout the year in the *Economist*, which has a very strong set of reporters covering China right now. See also John Garnaut, *The Rise and Fall of the House of Bo*, an e-book (Penguin, 2012); for a trenchant assessment of missed opportunities during Hu's ten years in power, see Ian Johnson, "China's Lost Decade," *New York Review of Books*, September 27, 2012.

On Chinese nationalism, good places to start in getting a sense of the range of scholarly approaches that have been taken to this complex subject are Jonathan Unger, editor, *Chinese Nationalism* (M. E. Sharpe, 1996); Prasenjit Duara, *The Global and the Regional in China's Nation-Formation* (Routledge, 2009); and Henrietta Harrison, *China: Inventing the Nation* (Oxford University Press, 2001). On contemporary nationalism and its complexities, see various contributions to works already mentioned, such as Rosen and Gries, *State and Society in 21st-Century China*; the Jensen and Weston volumes; Merkel-Hess et al., *China in 2008*; and Shah and Wasserstrom's *Chinese Characters*.

On energy and the environment, the best work is largely made available online through important projects such as the "China Green Project" (http://sites.asiasociety.org/chinagreen/links/), which is run through the Asia Society's Center on US–China relations that is headed by Orville Schell, who has traveled to and written about the PRC for well over three decades now; the inspiring "chinadialogue" bilingual website (http://www.chinadialogue.net/), which was launched by another veteran commentator on Chinese affairs, Isabel Hilton; and the Woodrow Wilson Center's "China Environment Forum" (http://www.wilsoncenter.org/index.cfm?topic_id=1421&fuseaction=topics.home), which is run by a specialist in PRC environmental issues, Jennifer Turner. On the issue of water, see Kenneth L. Pomeranz, "The Great Himalayan Watershed," *New Left Review*, July–August 2009. See also Christina Larson's chapter in *Chinese Characters*, "Yong Yang's Odyssey."

For smart and accessible takes on a range of issues associated with Chinese environmental and economic issues, see the writing that James Fallows has been doing in recent years in the *Atlantic*, a sampling of which can be found in *Postcards from Tomorrow Square: Reports from China* (Vintage, 2008). See also Jonathan Watts, *When a Billion Chinese Jump* (Scribner, 2010).

The value of thinking of China and the United States as sharing a great deal is emphasized in works such as Stephen Mihm, "A Nation of Outlaws: A Century Ago, That Wasn't China—It Was Us," *Boston Globe*, August 26, 2007; various contributions to Merkel-Hess et al., *China in 2008*; and Bruce Cumings's *Dominion from Sea to Sea: Pacific Ascendancy and American Power* (Yale University Press, 2009). See also Howard W. French, "Letter from China: China Could Use Some Honest Talk about Race," *International Herald Tribune*, July 31, 2009, http://www.nytimes.com/2009/08/01/world/asia/01iht-letter.html?partner=rssnyt&emc=rss, which usefully places side by side the riots that erupted in Detroit in July 1967 and those that took place in Xinjiang in July 2009.

INDEX